THE STORY OF
INDIA

Michael Wood
THE STORY OF
INDIA

BBC
BOOKS

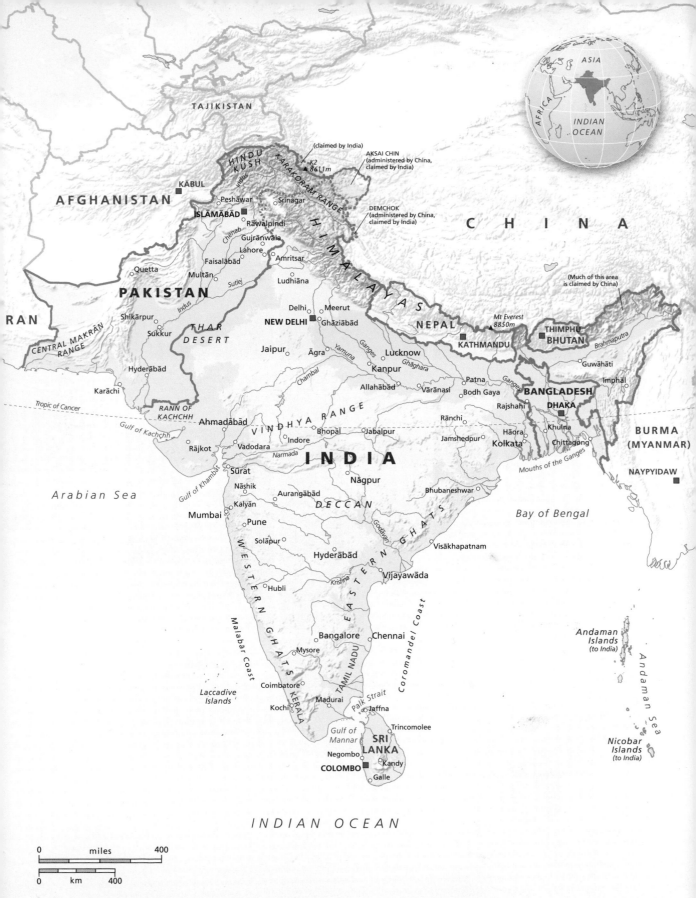

TAJIKISTAN

ASIA

AFRICA

INDIAN
OCEAN

HINDU KUSH

KĀBUL

AFGHANISTAN

ISLĀMĀBĀD

Peshāwar

Rāwalpindi

Chenab

Gujrānwāla

Lahore

Faisalābād

Amritsar

Multān

Ludhiāna

Quetta

Sutlej

PAKISTAN

Indus

(claimed by India)

K2
8611m

KARAKORAM RANGE

Srinagar

HIMALAYAS

AKSAI CHIN
(administered by China,
claimed by India)

DEMCHOK
(administered by China,
claimed by India)

CHINA

(Much of this area
is claimed by China)

Delhi

Meerut

NEW DELHI

Ghāziābād

NEPAL

Mt Everest
8850m

KATHMANDU

THIMPHU

BHUTAN

Brahmaputra

RAN

IRAN

Shikārpur

Sukkur

Hyderābād

Karāchi

CENTRAL MAKRĀN
RANGE

Jaipur

THAR
DESERT

Indus

Āgra

Yamuna

Ganges

Lucknow

Ghāghara

Kanpur

Chambal

Allahābād

Vārānasi

Patna

Bodh Gaya

Ganges

Guwāhāti

Imphāl

BANGLADESH

Rājshāhi

DHAKA

Tropic of Cancer

Gulf of Kachchh

RANN OF
KACHCHH

Ahmadābād

VINDHYA RANGE

Bhopāl

Jabalpur

Rānchi

Jamshedpur

Hāora

Khulna

Kolkata

Chittagong

BURMA
(MYANMAR)

Rājkot

Vadodara

Indore

Narmada

INDIA

Nāgpur

NAYPYIDAW

Sūrat

Gulf of Khambāt

Nāshik

Kalyān

Aurangābād

DECCAN

Bhubaneshwar

Mouths of the Ganges

Mumbai

Pune

Solāpur

Hyderābād

Godāvari

Visākhapatnam

Arabian Sea

WESTERN GHATS

Hubli

Krishna

Vijayawāda

EASTERN GHATS

Bay of Bengal

Andaman
Islands
(to India)

Bangalore

Mysore

Chennai

Coromandel Coast

Malabār Coast

Coimbatore

TAMIL NADU

KERALA

Madurai

Palk Strait

Kochi

Jaffna

Laccadive
Islands

Gulf of
Mannar

Trincomolee

Andaman Sea

SRI
LANKA

Negombo

Kandy

Nicobar
Islands
(to India)

COLOMBO

Galle

INDIAN OCEAN

0   miles   400

0   km   400

Introduction

THIS BOOK HAS COME OUT of a long attachment to India – an attachment filled with deep respect and admiration, but most of all love for India and its cultures. I have made twenty or thirty journeys to the subcontinent during the last three decades, and feel that in some ways my life has become enmeshed with India. Those journeys have so often made me think what a great privilege it is to be welcomed into another culture and to spend time in it, especially one so rich and diverse and perennially illuminating. My wife and I fell in love in India and were married there; our children have Indian names. We have travelled together in India as a family, and some of our most vivid memories are associated with the children when they were young: celebrating Pongal, the spring festival in the traditional household of Tamil friends; travelling the south by local bus to visit the old shrines of the Cavery delta; or, most memorably perhaps, staying with friends in a tent in the middle of the *Kumbh Mela* of 2001, the greatest human gathering on Earth – not to mention escaping afterwards to semolina pudding and fruit cake at our favourite little Parsee hotel in Allahabad.

But this is also a book by a historian. I have been travelling the world for forty years, most of that time working as a historian, writing books and making films, nearly a hundred of them, on travel, history and adventure (sometimes, as when we followed in the steps of Alexander over the Hindu Kush, all three at once). I have filmed with traditional civilizations in the Americas and Africa, in the great Old World civilizations of Iraq, Egypt, Iran and China, and have been lucky enough to see at first hand the incredible beauty, richness and diversity of human life on Earth. If there is a uniting theme in these experiences, it is the continuance of the past in our present. It is almost a truism that we live in a time when human identities – civilizations, cultures, tribes, individuals – are being erased everywhere across the globe; identities built up often over thousands of years and lost in just a few generations. When you travel you see, no less than with the environment, landscapes, climates and species, that modernity and globalization are rubbing out human differences too, the intricate web of languages, customs, music and stories that makes us who we are. We may be the last generation to see many of these things still alive. But it seems to me that nowhere on Earth can you find all human histories, from the Stone Age to the global village, still thriving, as you can in India. And that is the big story told in this book.

India became a free nation only sixty years ago, but in a real sense it has existed for thousands of years. The story of India is a tale of incredible drama, great inventions, enormous diversity, phenomenal creativity and the very biggest ideas. But it is also the history of one of the world's emerging powers. Today the population of the subcontinent as a whole – India, Pakistan and Bangladesh – is currently 1.5 billion, more than a fifth of all the world's people, and India itself will soon overtake China as the world's most populous country. India has twenty-two official languages (including English), and 400 smaller tongues and dialects: as a medieval Indian writer noted proudly, 'the people of Asia, the Mongols, the Turks and the Arabs get tongue-tied speaking our Indian languages, but we Indians can speak any language of the world as easily as a shepherd tends his sheep'. India, no doubt, has always been polylingual. It has also always been pluralist: its great regional cultures are civilizations in themselves (Tamil alone, to give one example, has a literature going back to the third century BC – richer and older than that of most western European nations). And that pluralism and diversity imbue everything from large to small. Indian society is made up of nearly 5000 castes and communities, each with its own rules, customs and stories. India gave birth to four world religions, and, along with its legendary 33 million gods, has a bewildering plethora of sects and subsects. It is also the second largest Muslim country on Earth, and the subcontinent as a whole has half of all Muslims in the world. India welcomed Christianity long before Europe embraced it, and has welcomed adherents of many other faiths, including Jews and Parsees (the Zoroastrians of Iran), as refugees from persecution.

And now, as the brief hegemony of the West is coming to an end, India, with all this amazing diversity, is rising again. Historical economists conjecture that India's GDP was the largest in the world until around 1500, when it was overtaken by China, only for both to be eclipsed in the age of the European empires when the centre of history shifted away from the landmass of Asia to the western European seaboard, transformed by the wealth of the New World. By 1900 both China and India had sunk to generating a tiny percentage of the world's wealth (in India's case, less than 3 per cent). For the first forty-five years after Independence in 1947, the Indian government followed a protectionist policy, loyal to the ideals of its founders, liberal socialists, but also Gandhians, espousing self-sufficiency, non-alignment and non-violence. Only in the last fifteen years has India followed China's lead in terms of growth. The chief factor in today's global world is sheer population, but mastery of information technology, skill in mathematics, and technical and linguistic skills are all playing their part, along with the widespread use of English as a lingua franca, and the size, spread and influence of the Indian diaspora. Leading financial analysts now predict that on present trends India's GDP will overtake that of the USA in the late 2030s. The twenty-first century, then, is seeing the history of the great ancient civilizations of Asia return to centre stage.

India's modern transformation started later than China's, and without the massive state-directed focus of that country. India also faces many problems, especially with social inequalities, rural poverty, overpopulation and environmental degradation. But India has immense advantages. It is an open society and a vibrant democracy, with formidable practical and language skills, and, as a civilization that has attempted to be pluralist and tolerant over a vast period of time, can draw on huge cultural resources from its past. The age-old life goals of Indian civilization – *artha* (worldly wealth and success), *kama* (pleasure and love), *dharma* (virtue) and *moksha* (knowledge and liberation) – are still major forces in people's lives, rich and poor, and, it seems to me, will be for the foreseeable future. Despite difficulties and setbacks, the establishment and acceptance of a dynamic working democracy has been a remarkable achievement over last sixty years: and it is a democracy that has many things to teach us all.

This book is a traveller's-eye view of the history of India, a brief and selective account of the country from the deep past to the present, highlighting some of the key moments and key themes in its story. Inevitably, it is only an introduction: the history of India is so vast, so rich and complex, that to contain even its outline in one volume is barely possible. Working there intensively over the last eighteen months has been a wonderful experience, seeing something of the latest exciting phase of India's amazing story; and on a personal level, I can only express my profound gratitude to all the people who gave us their time and their knowledge on the way. I leave the last word to the fourteenth-century Indian poet Amir Khusro: he was a Muslim, he wrote in Persian, and his ancestry was Turkic, but he counted himself the luckiest man alive to have been born in India, and to have India as his motherland.

> How exhilarating is the atmosphere of India!
> There cannot be a better teacher than the way of life of its people.
> If any foreigner comes by, he will have to ask for nothing
> Because they treat him as their own,
> Play an excellent host and win his heart,
> And show him how to smile like a flower.

1
Origins and Identity

THE RAIN HAS STOPPED, and the canopy of palms on the steep slope behind the house is drenched and dripping; dark green fronds glisten in the last light. Outside my room I can hear the roar of the undertow and the crash of breakers along the reef at the mouth of the bay. On the beach towards the lighthouse, knots of people are strung along the edge of the water watching the sunset. The monsoon sky is clearing now, and a golden light is spreading over the Arabian Sea. I'm stand-ing on the balcony of a lodging house on the Kerala coast near the southern tip of India. On the table are maps, guidebooks, a traveller's clutter. In the last few days we've come south down the coast from Calicut, through Cranganore and Cochin, along palm-fringed beaches under the red cliffs of Varkala, down the narrow strip between the sea and the forested foothills of the Western Ghats, the spine of India. A tourist resort like this might seem an unlikely place to begin a tale about the great migrations of the past, but this was the route taken by the first humans out of Africa perhaps 80,000 years ago: it's the first journey in Indian history.

Beachcombers

They were beachcombers, making their way barefoot down India's long, surf-beaten shores, driven as human beings always have been by chance and necessity. But also, surely, by curiosity, that most human of qualities. In only a few thousand years they skirted the Indian Ocean from the Horn of Africa to Cape Comorin on India's southern tip, and on to the Andamans, Indonesia and Australasia. Sea levels

then were lower: the pale blue shelf around India that can be seen so clearly from space is the old shoreline, lost 20,000 years ago when the sea began to rise. Back then there was a land bridge to Sri Lanka, and North and South Andaman were all one island, but right around the Indian Ocean the beachcombers' modern descendants have picked up faint traces of their ancestors' passage. Even now, small pockets of aboriginal peoples still survive around its shores. Opposite the Horn of Africa, humankind's first crossing-point out of the continent, the white beaches of Yemen, strewn with crimson coral, were their first stopping places. Along this coast their campsites have yielded Middle Palaeolithic tools, similar to those from the African Middle Stone Age. Across the Persian Gulf, on the coast of Pakistan too, in one of the most inhospitable landscapes on Earth, are the Makran people, who also have a very ancient strand in their DNA. (They were probably the nomadic population described by Alexander's Greeks in the fourth century BC as ichthyophagoi, or fish eaters, the most primitive people the Greeks met on the whole of their journey.)

Continuing around the ocean shore, in the forested hills of southern India, relatively undisturbed till the modern world, are pockets of tribal peoples who may also be descended from those very first beachcombers who came out of Africa. Long before the modern breakthrough with the Human Genome Project, their cultures and their African appearance had marked them out from the people surrounding them. British district gazetteers recorded their names: the Kadar, Paniyan and Korava, the Yanadi Irula, Gadaba and Chenchu. Older than the Dravidian speakers around them, they remain distinct, self-contained, outside the caste system of Hindu India.

Over the hills in Tamil Nadu I have arranged to meet Professor Pitchappan, a geneticist from Madurai University. He's made an extraordinary discovery working among the Kallar tribal people here. He's found traces of the ancestral mitochondrial DNA and Y chromosomes from the earliest genetic heritage of India. By chance, his team tested a man called Virumandi and discovered that he carries the M130 gene from the first wave of migrations of modern humans out of Africa. To their surprise, they subsequently discovered that Virumandi's whole village has M130 – carried down by isolation, by the strictures of the caste system, and by endogamy: the Kallar practice of first cousin marriage, the oldest and most characteristic form of kin marriage in southern India.

'There were at least two early waves of migration,' Professor Pitchappan tells me. 'We think spoken language only developed later – maybe only 10,000 or 15,000 years ago. Language, of course, is not the same as ethnicity. Language is easily adopted. And the same is true with religion too. Compared with custom, kin relations and so on, it's a surface layer, just a belief system: you believe in your system, your gods, whatever you feel like. It is for this reason that I believe India has become such a cosmos of humanity with all its diversity, but still unity.'

'Is that what makes you an Indian, then?' I ask.

'Well, probably,' he laughs. 'More a human being. A human being all the more, I would say.'

Despite all the waves of history, these people have remained in isolated groups since that original long walk. It is an incredibly exciting scientific breakthrough of the last few years, to begin to pin down such deep identities. And the professor even thinks that those first beachcombers provided the basis for the genetic inheritance of the rest of us. In other words, the world was populated from here: 'If Adam came from Africa, Eve came from India.' Mother India indeed!

It was a dizzying vista at the start of a journey through Indian history. And Kerala is a great place to understand the later layers of human culture in India. Spared violence, war and mass migrations, the modern horrors of population exchanges and ethnic cleansing, people came here as peaceful immigrants or traders. Its beautiful landscape and climate, its fertility and productivity made it a desirable stopping point throughout history. Its little harbours were the landfall of Hippalos the Greek, the Chinese admiral Zheng He and Vasco da Gama, who sailed here around the Cape in 1492. And then there are the lesser people we will meet in these pages: Greek and Roman merchants in the spice trade, Muslim Arab traders from the Gulf, Chinese immigrants who left their spidery nets fringing the Kerala backwaters. You see it in the architecture too: Syrian Christian basilicas, pillared Jewish synagogues, baroque Portuguese spice warehouses, the overgrown ruins of the British and Dutch East India companies, and now the tourist havens of Varkala and Kovalam served by budget package flights into Trivandrum. All are part of the ceaseless movement and intermixing of humanity that is the story of India.

Here you see a reality that happens not through war but through peace; the waves of people, cultures and religions that all make India what it is today. India may have hundreds of languages and thousands of castes, but here in a small area you see what that means on a human scale: incredible diversity, yet unity. On that conundrum we will have more to say.

Between 3000 and 4000 years ago a new wave of migrants came into India from central Asia. Some of them moved into the south in the last millennium BC. They brought their Vedic rituals and their worship of Agni, the god of fire, but over time, the gods and rituals of the indigenous peoples were assimilated, and this was the synthesis out of which today's Indian religions emerged. They called themselves 'Aryans' (the Sanskrit word for 'noble ones'), a term much abused in modern times by Nazis and other racial fundamentalists. Although most of the immigrants intermixed, their high-caste priests, or Brahmins, practised separation, handing down the ancient rituals and taboos.

India is a land of miracles. Here in Kerala anthropologists and district officers of the nineteenth century recorded a sect of Brahmins called *nambudiri*, who regarded themselves as the purest Aryans, and whose rituals were an ancient amalgam of the Aryan religion and indigenous rites, preserved zealously over thousands of years. At that time they still performed the most elaborate of all rituals, that to the god of fire. It took twelve days, some of them continuing right through the night. The last time that this twelve-day rite took place was more than thirty years ago; but this year, at the behest of a wealthy patron, a shorter version will be performed. It is, so far as we know, the oldest surviving ritual of mankind.

ABOVE

Agni, the god of fire: the sacrificial fire and the hearth were central to the rituals of the Vedic Indians; wooden panel, south India, 17th century.

Sounds from prehistory

Huge crowds jostle for a glimpse as fires send sparks high into the night sky. There are two specially built enclosures with altars, covered by rattan roofs. The biggest contains a large brick altar constructed in the shape of a bird with spread wings. Among a dozen officiating priests – young and old, fathers and sons – the chief priest sits on a black antelope skin, his head covered. He and his wife (here, unlike in mainstream Hinduism, women play a role), along with the other priests, may not leave the enclosure for the duration of the ritual. There are blood sacrifices, milk offerings to the Asvins (the divine boy twins who ride the winds), and a sacred

Rites to Agni, the god of fire. An ancient endogamous clan, the nambudiri *Brahmins are famous for their meticulous performance of some of humanity's oldest rituals; one of which, it has been speculated, may go back before human speech. Top left: teaching the mantras to the next generation. Top right: the performance takes place. Bottom: the huts are destroyed at the end in an act of purification.*

drink called *soma* is consumed, which is pressed from a mountain plant. For thousands of years these Brahminical rituals have been zealously guarded and never shared with the outside world; and this is especially true of the mantras. These magical formulas can take days to recite, only Brahmins can utter them, and they have been passed down orally from father to son, with exact accuracy, over a vast period of time.

Mantras still exist in many societies. They have spread in historical times from India to China, Tibet, the Far East and Indonesia. They are a part of the archaic past of mankind, but no culture has assigned more importance to them than that of India. They work on the emotions, the physiology and the nervous system; along with yoga, they are a way of achieving a heightened mental and physical state. Representations of figures on seals from the Bronze Age show men sitting in a yogic posture: it is probably one of the oldest obsessions of Indian culture.

Westerners were first able to get close to these practices and record them at a performance in 1975. But when they sat down to analyse them, to unpick their mystery, scholars were perplexed. During parts of the ritual there was no communication through ordinary language. The patterns of sounds that were recited – patterns that took years to learn and days to recite – clearly followed elaborate rules, but they had no meaning. In fact, meaning was something on which the Brahmins could offer no light. This was 'what was handed down'. The doing was all. What could be the purpose? How had they developed?

Two important ideas from other forms of human creativity can perhaps help us to approach this problem. The first is music: another way of organizing sounds

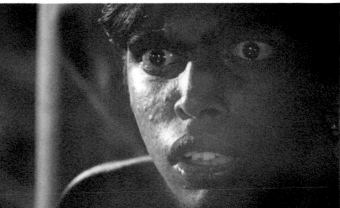

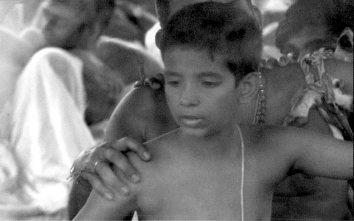

into an experience to create emotion. For music also has no meaning in itself; in other words, it is not capable of expressing anything. The second is ritual, which also need have no meaning. Hence, meaning need not have been important in the early roots of religion. It was only later in human history, through sacred texts and stories, that humans tried to give a rational explanation, a system, for their most archaic practices.

When experts analysed recordings of the mantras they were mystified. The patterns had no analogue in human culture. Not even music in the end was helpful, although mantras do have refrains, cycles and triplets. The breakthrough was only made possible by the development of computer technology. Patterns of mantras from the twelve-day Agni ritual recorded in 1975 were put on to a computer, and computer analysis showed that the nearest analogue of these sound sequences was birdsong. An astonishing conclusion might follow: the possibility that the performance of such patterns of sounds is older than human language, a remnant of a pre-linguistic stage when sound was used in a purely syntactical or ritual manner. *Homo sapiens*, it is now suspected, developed speech only in the last 50,000 years, since the migration from Africa, and perhaps much more recently. But we know from the animal kingdom that there was ritual before there was speech – when sound and gesture are combined in 'ritual' behaviour. If so, the combination of ritual with pre-speech sounds perhaps takes us to the dawn of humanity, the beginning of ritual and religion and science.

At the end of the great ritual, the two specially constructed houses are set alight and crumple into their own flames. Red fire licks up the bamboo scaffolding,

consuming the thatch and flaring into the night sky. Swirling showers of sparks fly as the structures crash down, firelight catching dark fronds of palm forest. At the start of our journey, then, it's clear that India may be leaping ahead in the global economy, predicted to overtake the United States in the 2030s, but here is a modern state in the twenty-first century that has preserved habits from its deepest past, and from that of humanity as a whole. It is nothing less than a laboratory of the human race.

The long, slow rise of humanity

The story of early humanity is still to be written, but with the new genetic discoveries, dramatic changes in our view of the human past are being made even as I write. What we can say is that over the first tens of thousands of years we are dealing with tiny numbers of people – the hunter-gatherers circling the fringes of the subcontinent and moving up river valleys to avoid the arid, fissured massif of the Deccan that dominates India's geography. The gene pool was replenished by several later migrations. The world that emerged in the Middle Stone Age already had many language families. The population of India at that time had a hard existence. Excavations at Mahada have turned up the skeletons of one community of hunter-gatherers; they were almost all around twenty years old, one was around thirty, none was over forty. Their material life, though, is depicted with brilliant vivacity on Late Middle Stone Age paintings in the caves at Bhimbetka, which show the communal animal hunts, the killings and propitiatory ceremonies of these hunter-gatherers.

BELOW

The oldest religion? Terracotta of the mother goddess from Mohenjo-Daro from c.2000 BC with an elaborate headdress. Similar figures are found in the Indus valley from the 7th millennium BC.

Of the early gods we know little, but looking at the dancing deity at Bhimbetka with his bangles and trident, one can't help but recall the image of the dancing Shiva seen on pilgrim posters today. The mother goddess too, with her full figure and 'eyes like fish', represents an ancient and irrepressible current in the Indian imagination, which has never been forsaken in the face of the monotheisms of Islam and Christianity, nor by the Westernization of modern times. What is certain too is that the symbols of procreative power – the stone lingam and yoni (male and female principles) – that are found in the worship of Shiva come out of the deep past. Not so long ago, when archaeologists excavated a shrine near Allahabad, south of the Ganges valley, a broken yoni stone from around 14,000 years ago was instantly recognized by today's villagers. These aspects of the indigenous culture of India are part of the givenness of the deep past, which is shared by all Indians, whatever their ancestry, language or religion.

My beginning is necessarily impressionistic. The passage of time is vast, and there are hundreds of generations about which, as yet, little is known and much is still to be discovered. The tale of the hunter-gatherers is the tale of the long, slow rise of humanity, the gradual, imperceptible tracing of India's early languages, beliefs, ritual traditions and gods. A period of tens of thousands of years has left its legacy in the indigenous peoples who still live all over the subcontinent. But then, starting in western Asia about 10,000 years ago, the first signs of settled cultures emerged in villages with agriculture, trade, metalworking and handicrafts. Whether changes in the monsoon regime helped bring this about is not yet clear, though it is suspected that climate change and a much wetter annual cycle helped bring migrants into the subcontinent from the west. In the culture of this time, on the edge of the Afghan plateau around 7000 BC, are the seeds of Indian civilization. And among the most important archaeological discoveries of the last hundred years was the breakthrough made out in the wilds of Baluchistan.

Baluchi dawn

The road from the Indus at Sukkur heads northwest towards Quetta and the Afghan border up the Bolan river. This is an ancient travel route between Iran and India, used by migrants for thousands of years. It is more ancient, so the archaeology suggests, than the Khyber Pass. You go through Jacobabad, now the site of a fortified US base for the war in Afghanistan. Founded by a British general, John

BELOW

The river Indus, which gave India its name. Rising near Mount Kailash in Tibet, it was encountered by Indo–Aryans below Khyber. The root of the name in Persian Hind means 'boundary stream'.

proclaim the new act for the protection of women: women's rights are the next big battle in a country caught between its Islamic heritage and its burgeoning modernity. Huge new motorway service stations stand like palaces in great, glistening pools of light, and sprawling industrial towns dot the road from Lahore to Multan. This is the new Pakistan, where dramatic modernization has occurred in the ten years since I last came this way. Pakistan is now the sixth most populous country in the world. It was divided from India in 1947 by nationalism and religion, but it is still a part of the subcontinent, still an inheritor of Indian civilization.

It is dark by the time we pass Sahiwal and leave the main road. We cross a huge irrigation canal as wide as a river, the air suddenly cold now, then on to a deserted country road, the occasional bus rattling past, horn blaring. We are now on a much more ancient road. This is the old main highway between Lahore and Multan, the artery of the Punjab for thousands of years, right back to when the Punjab was the heartland of Indian civilization. Along this stretch of the plain the mounds of ruined ancient cities are as abundant as they are in Iraq. Then the road sign appears in Urdu and English: Harappa.

Our headlights momentarily light up a ruined Mughal caravanserai and a mud fort. A bunch of sleepy camels chews patiently. This was the road taken by a British deserter, James Lewis, aka Charles Masson, the first outsider to describe Harappa. On his way south one night in 1828 he camped at dusk and saw 3 miles of walls along undulating wooded mounds by an old bed of the river Ravi. Amid thick 'jangal' – the tangled forest of rakh trees that once covered all this part of the Punjab – he noticed ancient pipal trees, which were sacred in the old Hindu religion. Masson saw that dominating the site, was 'a ruinous brick castle … an irregular rocky height crowned with the remains of buildings', walls and towers still 'remarkably high, though long deserted, that exhibit the ravages of time and decay'. What he had found was a ruined medieval city in the last stage of its life, built on a great, ancient mound 50–60 feet high, with a core of giant brick defences, berms and revetments, huge ruinous bastions like the mud-brick *qalats* (fortified villages) still to be seen in Afghanistan and the Khyber region. The last major construction on the site had been a Sikh fort in the eighteenth century. Making his way up on to the mound, Masson inspected an abandoned brick mosque of the Mughal period, with pointed windows. The city had largely died out when the Ravi moved its bed in the Middle Ages. But Masson heard another story from his local guides – the legend of 'a great city that was destroyed by a particular visitation of Providence, brought down by the lust and crimes of the Sovereign'. What he could not know was that the city in fact went back over 5000 years.

Finally, we reach the site. The dig hut is in a grove of trees, nestling under a giant banyan. Muffled figures come out and help to unload our gear. The joint

US–Pakistani archaeology team are not here at the moment, and the site custodian has let us take over the bedroom, with its three bedsteads. Wisps of pale mist curl across the garden on to the veranda, and Tanweer, the expedition cook, has swathed himself in a blanket against the cool, dank night air. In the kitchen we wolf down some rice, vegetables and daal, and hot black tea. Hassan, the archaeologist in charge of the site, has stayed to greet us and comes over in a quilted jacket, hands stuffed into his pockets: 'Welcome to Harappa!'

We make the dormitory as comfy as possible, stacking the camera gear and unrolling our sleeping-bags, while we try to swat the mosquitoes. Masson was plagued with them in 1828, 'swarms of tiny antagonists' he called them, to the point where he got up in the middle of the night and rode 12 miles to Chichawatna, abandoning his camp after his tantalizing first glimpse of Harappa. A pity, because he never had time to sketch it and leave us one of the excellent drawings he did of other lost sites in the Indus region and Afghanistan. Less than thirty years later what Masson saw was destroyed by British railway contractors, who were laying the track from Multan to Lahore, spreading the tentacles of empire. Finding a ready supply of burnt bricks, they demolished the citadel, quarrying the bricks for ballast

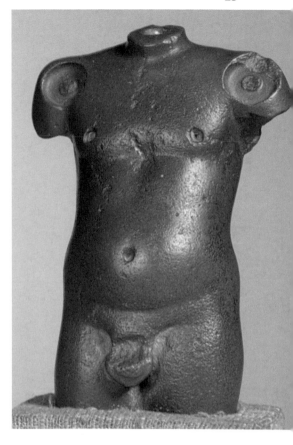

for hundreds of miles of track. From the debris they retrieved fine pottery and strange seals, which eventually came into the hands of the head of the newly formed Indian Archaeological Survey, General Alexander Cunningham. On the seals Cunningham saw an unknown system of writing. Although he could not have known it then, they came from a lost civilization. This would only be revealed in the 1920s. Then, in just a few years, the history of Indian civilization would be entirely rewritten. As the British archaeologist John Marshall wrote:

> Not often has it been given to archaeologists, as it was given to
> Schliemann at Tiryns and Mycenae, or to Stein in the deserts of
> Turkestan, to light upon the remains of a forgotten civilization.
> It looks, however, at the moment, as if we were on the threshold
> of such a discovery in the plains of the Indus …

The excavations developed slowly, initially on a small scale. Eventually, under the ground at Harappa, untouched by the railway contractors, the huge brick

ABOVE

A miniature red sandstone torso from c. 2000 BC: a rare piece of figural sculpture from the Indus civilization.

LEFT

Harappa today. Its enormous medieval walls and ancient revetments were quarried by Victorian railway contractors. All that remained was, as here, below the surface of the ground.

Seals from the Indus, tiny masterpieces of glyptic art. Top: an Indian hump-backed bull with huge dewlaps. Bottom: a 'unicorn' standing in front of an altar. The unknown system of writing may be an early relative of the Dravidian languages spoken in south India.

revetments of a fortified citadel would be uncovered, and on the west side, where the railway contractors had left off their depredations, a cutting through the citadel wall would expose a canyon of bricks, still solid, 50 feet deep. It was immediately apparent that the place had been a great city on the scale of the urban centres of the Near East. The finds at Harappa, and at Mohenjo-Daro in Sind in late 1923, took place in the same period of eighteen months or so that saw Leonard Woolley excavate the tombs of Ur in Iraq, and, of course, Howard Carter's discovery of the tomb of Tutankhamun. Although the finds at Harappa were less spectacular in terms of artefacts, the significance of the dig went way beyond either.

The discoveries here and at Mohenjo-Daro represented the beginning of the history of the Indian subcontinent, taking its cities back to 3000 BC – before the Pyramids of Giza. Until the dig at Harappa, it had been widely believed in Europe that civilization in India was a foreign import, that it was the creation of the classical civilizations of the Mediterranean, and the Judaeo-Christian tradition of the Near East, with a little help from their ancient predecessors in Egypt and Babylon. The Indian Brahmin priests, however, had long asserted that their own civilization went back thousands of years. Their tradition of the great war in the epic poem the *Mahabharata* took it back 5000 years, while their traditional genealogies, the ancient texts known as Puranas, contained king lists that, if taken literally, would take Indian chronology back to the Bronze Age. In the eighteenth century some Western thinkers had been prepared to take these ideas at face value and to seek connections (however misguided they might seem now) with ancient Egypt and the Bible. But the colonial orientalist project tended in the main to dismiss Hindu thought as superstition and fetishism, a more 'primitive' stage of culture, which needed to be emancipated by the science, reason and religion of the West. No one believed that an indigenous Indian civilization could go back far before the classical civilizations of the Mediterranean. Back in 1924, though, Marshall could have had no idea how far back Harappa might go, just that it was 'older than anything known in India', and (with uncanny intuition) that it must be indigenous, and 'as distinctive of the region as that of the Pharaohs was distinctive of the Nile'. My mind whirling, I closed his account and finally fell asleep with a last feeble swat at the descendants of Masson's mosquitoes.

A little after 5 a.m. Tanweer wakes us with hot water and black coffee under the huge banyan behind the house, which stands like a massive, aged sentinel from a time when this region was still India. The first mauve light brings shapes out of the mist and reveals a white dusting over the salt-encrusted landscape. Cheered by the coffee, we walk out on to the site, past spoil heaps and the stumps of walls, with burnt bricks littered everywhere. We watch the sun rise from the top of the site surrounded by feathered trees, all that remains of Harappa's rakh forest. The atmosphere is still and ghostly white. Long plumes of pale smoke rise from brick kilns, whose spindly chimneys can be seen a few miles off, spreading flat across the fields to the west along the horizon. Brick was the great building medium of the Harappan civilization, and in the Punjab for thousands of years. The brick kilns must have been working overtime back then when these giant cities were built by thousands of workers, who created huge brick-foundation platforms and giant berms and bunds to fight the unremitting floods. From our vantage point, we look over the old bed of the Ravi, which once flowed under the city walls, and we can hear the village rising, ox-carts beginning to trundle down the banks of the irrigation ditches as the muezzin calls the faithful to prayer.

The joint Pakistani and US team is currently engaged in a new dig. Rolling back the frontiers of knowledge still further, it is now possible to trace the links with the earlier Baluchi sites excavated by the French in Mehrgahr, and to put the Indus cities in the context of a 10,000-year history of civilization in the subcontinent. Mark Kenoyer, the American on the team, is a remarkable man. Born in India, he speaks four native languages fluently, and it is his experience of the life lived rather than of books read that informs his insights into the continuities of Indian civilization. I had caught up with him in the UK before our journey, and he told me:

> Even in today's Harappa you can see the legacy of the Indus cities reflected in the layout of houses and settlements, and in the traditional arts and crafts, which still use the old techniques. We have even found little clay toys that are identical to the ones made in the Punjab until today. These are the living links between the people of the Indus cities and the later population of Pakistan and India.

Mohenjo-Daro: the mound of the dead

About 150 miles below Harappa the rivers of the Punjab join to become the Indus, from which the name India (*Hind* in Persian) is derived. The sensational finds in the early 1920s showed that, like the Nile and the Euphrates, the Indus river valley was home to a great early civilization. The Indus, like the other Himalayan rivers, is swollen by the spring snow melt, and above all by the summer monsoon. Before the modern construction of barrages, a million tons of silt a day were carried past to be deposited on the riverbed or at the delta mouth. This led to a progressive aggregation of the plain, which has pushed the mouth 70 miles into the Arabian Sea since the time of Alexander the Great. Sometimes the huge weight of silt forces the river to break its banks and find another course. A famous passage in the writings of Strabo about Alexander's expedition describes how they saw 'a deserted zone which contained more than a hundred towns with all the villages dependent on them. The Indus having quit its bed, had moved across to another bed on its left bank, a deeper one, and poured into it like a cataract. No longer irrigated, the region formerly inundated on its right bank, whose bed it had left, now found itself high and dry above the level of the annual floods.'

After the initial discoveries at Harappa, Marshall and his Indian colleagues now looked for an untouched site in this southern region of the Indus and in 1923 they chose a promising site 400 miles to the south in the arid plains of Sind. Here was a vast ruin still crowned by a Buddhist stupa of the Kushan period, the time of the Romans in the West. Mohenjo-Daro, the 'mound of the dead', lay on a ridge in the floodplain known to locals as 'the Island'. Although the ridge is now deeply buried by the annual flooding that covered the plain even in Indus times, it must have been much more prominent during the prehistoric period, with the early city standing on a massive artificial platform high above the plain and entirely surrounded by water during periods of flood. Despite the ravages of time, and of floods that had cut a great swathe across the site, it was still huge, by far the largest of the Indus cities, extending over 1 square mile, with widespread mounds and outlying suburbs.

On the mound whole sectors of housing had survived in good condition, with deep, brick-lined wells, and latrines at the end of every block, which were connected to sewers large enough to walk in. Everything was planned with strange regularity: 'Anyone walking through it for the first time,' said John Marshall, 'might fancy himself surrounded by the ruins of some present-day working town in Lancashire.' The most imposing part of Mohenjo-Daro was the Great Bath, which was in the citadel. It is a finely built, brick-lined bathing tank 40 feet long, with a large building on the side variously interpreted as a temple, or even some kind of 'college'. Not unnaturally, the excavator, Rakhhaldas Banerji, suspected some connection with later ritual bathing tanks in Indian temples. The citadel is an impressive construction built on a high mound of dirt, with an artificial brick platform that it is estimated would have taken 10,000 workers about thirteen months to create. This upper city rises from the floodplain, covering an area about 600 x 1200 feet. An ancient brick bund or flood barrier 4 miles to the east diverted the main flow of the Indus away from the city.

In its heyday, Mohenjo-Daro would have dominated the riverine trade networks moving from the coast to the northern Indus plain, as well as the trade routes leading to the passes in the Bolan valley to the west. One of today's excavators of Mohenjo-Daro,

BELOW

Mohenjo-Daro style: a terracotta pot from c. 2000 BC with a painting of a goat, one of the animals domesticated here from the 7th millennium BC.

Michael Janssen, thinks the empire must have been linked by boat. 'Life in Mohenjo-Daro was semi-amphibious. For four to five months of the year the plain of Sind was a vast sheet of water. The cities were linked by river, and there must have been a revolution in boat transport to create what looks like a gigantic network; this may also help to explain the homogenization of the material culture.' Close to Mohenjo-Daro, on the Indus at Sukkur, you can still see these kinds of boat – great wooden vessels with ornate sterns some 80–90 feet long, carved wood deckhouses, and huge sails – just as depicted on Indus seals. Flat-bottomed, to cope with a wide, shallow river, strong current and frequent winds, they are a living continuity with the Bronze Age.

If you could have glimpsed it from the air, Mohenjo-Daro in its heyday would have been a vast, irregular hexagon, the suburbs protected by enormous brick embankments against the river inundations. The main part of the city was a warren of houses, overlooked by the citadel with its fine buildings. Imagine the burning Sindhi summers, with cotton awnings stretched over sun-baked courtyards and streets, just as one can see today; or the chill winters, with domestic wood fires sending myriad streamers of smoke lifting over the rooftops and swirling in spindrifts across ink-black monsoon skies, while carved boats with great cotton sails leave the jetties and head downriver towards the Gulf, with their cargoes of precious wood, elephant ivory, cotton and lapis lazuli.

ABOVE

Traditional boats on the Indus with their carved stern house and huge rudder are depicted on Indus seals. They carried goods up and down the Indus until very recently. But this ancient way of life is almost gone now. This picture was taken in 1996.

The Indus civilization

So a picture emerged with dramatic swiftness in the 1920s of the earliest civilization of India. It was bigger in area than Egypt and Mesopotamia or any other ancient civilization. We now know there were over 2000 major settlements, extending as far as the Oxus river in northern Afghanistan, some of which were big, planned cities on the Near Eastern model. Most of its mounds remain unexplored, including several huge ones near Harappa. Using data from Alexander's day, the Greek geographer Strabo, writing in the first century AD, said the Punjab had 5000 large settlements that deserved the Greek name *polis* (city). The old riverbeds here are still lined with great city mounds; and the dried-up Ghaggar-Hakra bed has 1500 prehistoric sites, some, like the untouched mound of Ganwerianwala, the same size as Mohenjo-Daro and Harappa. Not only were they vast, they were also populous. The size of the civilization is estimated at anywhere between 2 million and 5 million people, although no one knows for certain, and is surely a pointer to the fact that with nearly 1.5 billion people today, the Indian subcontinent is the most populous place on Earth, and it no doubt was in ancient world.

But who were the rulers? The archaeologists think that there are several perplexing clues. Mohenjo-Daro bears all the signs of a city that was willed into existence by some powerful person or group of people; a 'founder city', like, say, Alexandria. The streets were straight, laid out on a north–south and east–west grid.

The so-called 'priest king' of Mohenjo-Daro with his 'cloak of stars', arm ring and ornamental dot on his forehead. Whether this is a ruler, a priest, a merchant, or someone who was all three is not known.

The houses of brick on top of stone foundations seem to have been built to standard designs. Nearly all of them were connected to a city-wide drainage system, and each block had one or more water wells, but there are no great tombs as we find in, say, Egypt, Iraq or China, and no great palatial buildings. Yet although there is no material evidence for rulers, all around is indirect testimony to some kind of powerful, centrally directed organizing influence. Who oversaw foreign commerce by sea and regulated the system of weights? Who established the uniform sign system in the script? How to explain the apparently common religion, uniform pottery and coherent Indus style of artefacts over a period of 700 years, spanning nearly thirty generations? 'We have the strange situation of a complex ancient society without the ostentations of ideology or evidence of a focused leadership, like a king or queen,' says Mark Kenoyer. 'There's no real model in history for a civilization like this one.'

Strangest of all for the archaeologists is that they found no evidence of war and conflict. In Egypt and Mesopotamia war was the great occupation of Bronze Age rulers. In inscriptions and images on stelas, art and sculpture, war is the central theme. Here that is not the case. And did the ancient Greeks not say of Indians that they never waged aggressive war beyond India out of their own deep-rooted cultural aversion and 'their respect for justice'? Certainly they had fortified cities, but there are no images of war on the thousands of Indus seals, and no depiction of warfare, captive-taking or killing.

'Is it possible,' asks Mark Kenoyer, 'that in the long, gradual evolution of over 4000 years of local cultures before the age of cities, they worked out how to organize their settlements, interact with other communities, what to do with surpluses, how to pass on knowledge and how to resolve conflict? It's an intriguing idea that early India was different from other civilizations. The answer to that is that we don't know.'

Although the later history of India was often incredibly violent, it is clear that the idea of non-violence runs very deep in Indian thought, from the Buddha, the Jains, the Ashokan edicts and the Gupta kings through to Mahatma Gandhi, and it may not have been new in the fifth century BC. Jain culture in particular has very archaic features, and derives from the zone of the Indus civilization in Gujarat. But if anything like that were true, it would be unique in the violent history of humanity.

Why did the civilization collapse?

Towards 1800 BC, after 700 years of apparent stability, the Indus civilization collapsed and its cities were abandoned. Its disappearance, apparently leaving little trace, poses another big question: what led to its downfall? There have been many suggestions, including, as we shall see, outside invasion. But experts are now increasingly looking at climate change as a chief factor. In London I went to see Sanjiv Gupta, an expert in geology and hydrography at Imperial College. Sanjiv deals in aeons of geological time, in which a mere 4000 years is as yesterday. The level of analysis now possible in his field is staggering; for example, he can take grains of sand from a riverbed and tell us where they came from. At present he is looking at one of the most controversial questions in early Indian history – the possible existence of a great river system east of the Indus that dried up in the Bronze Age and that some identify with the legendary lost sacred river, the Saraswati. He is still formulating the questions he will ask when he can take an expedition on the ground.

On the screen in Sanjiv's office are satellite images of Rajasthan, different colours denoting sand-dunes, vegetation and the presence of water. He explains:

> The Punjab has many lost watercourses. Here rivers change course quite dramatically, and most of the big rivers have shifted by several miles, even in the last two or three thousand years. But the big question at the moment is whether there really *was* a lost river. Local oral traditions were noticed by the British in the nineteenth century, and several gazetteers pick up this idea of a lost river. The explorer Aurel Stein, searching for sites connected with Alexander the Great in the 1930s, took horses down the Beas, where he came upon a vast depression, up to 2 or 3 miles across. Now look at what we see with the satellite photos …

On the computer screen a montage joins three landsat images, and a dark, snaking line appears, stretching from northeast to southwest across the Rajasthani desert.

> Look at the dark line winding across Rajasthan before it loses itself in the sand-dunes of the Thar desert. There's definitely something there, though we need to go on the ground to confirm it. There are no habitation sites there today, but now look at this. We've computerized the main Bronze Age sites using information from Indian and Pakistani archaeologists, and data from surface surveys on both sides of the border. The Pakistani team tracked 1500 sites through the desert of Cholistan, and they all seem to map out a feature that connects with ours.

On the screen, a line of orange dots appears, clustering alongside the dark, snaking feature, all of them representing settlements from the Harappan civilization in its last phase, when we know the big cities, such as Harappa and Mohenjo-Daro, were still functioning. The feature seems to extend for over 90 miles of the Thar desert, from Rajasthan across the Pakistan border.

> We can go in and focus on individual places. Let's take one site. This one, 120 miles southeast of Harappa, is Kalibangan, excavated by Indian archaeologists in the 1970s. It's a major Harappan-period city and stands right on the dried-up bed you saw on the satellite imagery. Clearly, this once held water. In the Bronze Age Kalibangan was on a river, or a major seasonal source of water, and was an important centre of population. Now obviously, you couldn't have had all these sites

where there was no water, and the reason for their existence is the river whose drying up we can date pretty closely. So what happened to the people? Now look at this.

On the screen appears a new set of data: a series of green dots flashes up, spreading across from the area of the lost river to the plain of the river Ganges and the Jumna. The number of sites along the Indus has now declined, and they vanish altogether from the area of the presumed lost river; but many more have now appeared in the Ganges–Jumna doab (the tract of land lying between the two rivers). It looks like a massive shift of settlement and population.

'These green dots are the sites that were occupied after the end of the Indus cities. Those cities died out over a century or two around 1800 BC, including all the sites along the lost river; then these sites developed, moving eastwards into the upper Ganges and Jumna valleys, becoming the centre of the next phase of Indian civilization – indeed, right up until today.'

'So did they move due to environmental collapse or climate change?' I ask.

'Maybe there was a change in the monsoon regime,' says Sanjiv, 'but it certainly looks as if the amount of water on the Ghaggar-Hakra diminished, and that helped prompt the movement of people eastwards. It looks like it, but the only way to be sure is to go and examine the geology and sediment. To get accurate dating we have to get out on the ground.'

Clues from the lost river

Early British administrators were eye-witnesses to the last phase of these changes. The Thar district gazetteer of 1919 describes two absolutely distinct worlds: to the west were the rich alluvial plains of the Indus; to the east, sandy desert. The old gazetteers also give crucial information about the apparent lost river revealed on Sanjiv's landsat images. The lower course is called the Nara, which empties into the Rann of Kutch and joins up with the line on the satellite images. But the gazetteers also prove that it is not exactly true to say that all the water dried up. The course of the Nara flooded annually, and a century ago a district officer reported 'a carpet of evergreen grass with a dense tamarisk, kandi and babul jungle interspersed with large deep lakes running miles into sandhills, and having a perennial stream of water running through the valleys'. In the times of seasonal inundations this was almost all water. Of these lakes the greatest was the Maakhi Dhand, the haunt of outlaws and robbers who defied British forces in the 1890s. These lakes disappeared after the introduction of British irrigation works, but the description perhaps gives us an idea of what conditions might have been like here in the Bronze Age. Remarkably, this may find an echo in Indian myth. The earliest Sanskrit poetry, composed in the period after the Indus cities, mentions a big river that joined the sea east of the Indus; later legend says this river disappeared, but today it is still remembered as a goddess in the hierophany of Indian sacred rivers. Her name is Saraswati, 'river of lakes'.

So the lost river was real – an important centre of civilization during the Bronze Age. Perhaps it was never one great flowing stream like the rivers of the Punjab, but a series of lakes and channels subject to seasonal floods and periodic contractions throughout history. When sections dried up, or the flow diminished, large tracts of land dried up, and cities and settlements died. The mapping of literally thousands of sites of the Harappan civilization, and the population movement into the Ganges valley at the end of the Bronze Age, strongly suggest that the Indus civilization declined because of the abandonment of the cities, caused by environmental change that led to the shift of the lower courses of the Indus and the Punjab rivers, and the drying up of the Ghaggar-Hakra.

Now let's put the evidence together for the end of India's first great civilization. There were many causes of its decline, but modern archaeology suggests big changes occurred after some 700 years of stability in the Indus world. Mohenjo-Daro was badly flooded several times between 1900 and 1700 BC; the grand buildings on the citadel were subdivided into small houses and workshops; the great bath was built over. At Dholavira ordinary people moved into the public buildings. At Harappa there was overcrowding on the high mound; the drains were no longer cleared; the streets became clogged with rubbish, including dead animals, and were abandoned. There is also evidence for violence. Skeletons at Mohenjo-Daro were left in the streets; at Harappa reburials of disarticulated skeletons killed by violence suggest that the city had entered a time of uncertainty, as do the hoards of ornaments and jewels buried by their owners who never returned. At Lothal the harbour installations were burnt down; trade fell apart and long-distance commerce vanished altogether: evidence from Mesopotamia too suggests that trade with the Indus region dried up. And, of course, the written script ceased to be used, suggesting that the elite's structures of power had broken down. Although a population remained in the Indus valley, many were leaving the area and farming new lands on the Jumna and Ganges rivers. It was the end of a great era, but a long, slow decline rather than a cataclysm.

So the world of the Indus cities collapsed, and a sub-Indus culture emerged, mixing with new elements. But was the fall of cities accompanied by the arrival of newcomers, migrants or invaders? The question of newcomers is one of the biggest issues in Indian history today, massively controversial in recent years, with heavily politicized debates about Indian identity. The next phase of the story centres on one plain and incontrovertible fact: the speakers of the languages spoken across northern India to Bengal, languages that are first traceable after the end of the cities, are closely related to the family of languages across Eurasia known as Indo-European. Everyone agrees on this, but its significance is now bitterly contested. Many aspects of the argument are still shrouded in mystery, and there are many places this tale could begin, but one is Calcutta in the days of the East India Company.

The coming of the Aryans

In 1786 a British judge in Calcutta, Sir William Jones, made an extraordinary discovery. A Welshman and a brilliant linguist, who knew Greek, Latin and Persian (the last of these essential for a judge and administrator in Mughal India), Jones's great desire had been to learn Sanskrit, the language of the ancient Hindu texts and laws. Eventually, a Brahmin offered to teach him, and as he worked his way through the Sanskrit texts, he was fascinated to see close linguistic resemblances with Latin, Greek and modern Western languages. Some were obvious: for example, 'father', *pater* in Greek and Latin, is *pitar* in Sanskrit; likewise 'mother', *meter*, is *matar* in Sanskrit. Some links are intriguingly precise: the crucial word for 'horse' (*asva* in Sanskrit) is the same in Lithuanian, far away on the shores of the Baltic Sea. How could this have come about?

Jones announced his discovery in a lecture to the newly formed Asiatic Society of Bengal on 2 February 1786:

> The Sanskrit language, whatever be its antiquity, is of a wonderful structure; more perfect than the Greek, more copious than the Latin, and more exquisitely refined than either, yet bearing to both of them a stronger affinity, both in the roots of verbs, and in the forms of grammar, than could possibly have been produced by accident; so strong indeed, that no philologer could examine them all three without believing them to have sprung from some common source, which, perhaps, no longer exists.

Jones was not, in fact, the first to see the connection. From the sixteenth century earlier visitors, such as the English Jesuit Thomas Stevens, had seen the similarities of Sanskrit to Latin and Greek. What Jones did was to use this as evidence that the languages had a common root. He first speculated that India itself was the mother country, but he later came to believe that the language had come from outside – that Sanskrit was not indigenous to India, but had migrated into the subcontinent. Out of that idea in the nineteenth century came the theory of the coming of the Aryans.

no longer understood. Today it still has the same wording, whether in Kashmir, Orissa or Tamil Nadu; a more faithful transmission, then, than of some of the Greek and Roman classics. During the twentieth century the growing reliance on written texts at Vedic schools means that purely oral transmission has probably now died out, and the text taught today derives from written versions. Nonetheless, listening to a present-day recitation is rather like hearing a tape recording of what was first composed between 3000 and 4000 years ago.

Understanding the Rig-Veda, though, is another matter. It is a collection of notoriously riddling and difficult texts, full of inscrutable allusions, in very archaic language. The majority are hymns of praise and supplication addressed to the gods; many sing the delights of *soma*, the sacred drink; there are also battle songs that celebrate the crushing of enemies, and verses giving thanks in response to the gifts of chieftains (a well-known genre in Anglo-Saxon and Old Norse poetry too). As for the date, it's impossible to be exact, but one very important clue was unearthed in the 1920s. In the text of a treaty from the kingdom of Mitanni in northern Syria, datable to around 1380 BC, the names of the rulers, to scholars' great surprise, could be read perfectly as Sanskrit. The treaty also lists the Vedic gods Indra, Mitra and Varuna, in the very order in which they appear in a formulaic phrase in the Rig-Veda. The text also invokes the Nasdatya or Asvins, the heavenly twins who are very important in Vedic poems. Another Mitanni text, on chariots and horse training, written in the Indo-European language used by the rulers of Mitanni, is so close to Sanskrit in its numerals and technical terms that it is hard to imagine the languages of the Mitanni and the Aryans had been separated for very long. The mysterious Mitanni rulers were probably a warrior elite who came into northern Syria around 1700 BC and ruled what is now the area of Kurdistan. Their texts strongly suggest the early Rig-Vedic hymns came from a similar time, that is, not long before *c.*1400 BC. Further clues back this up. The Rig-Veda hymns describe a bronze-using world (iron first appears in India around 1200 BC); their authors seem unaware of great cities, such as Mohenjo-Daro, and know only of ruins whose people have fled, 'driven away by Agni, the god of fire'. All this combines to suggest that the bulk of hymns were composed after the Indus civilization. This gives us a triangulation: the composition of the hymns perhaps spreads over a few centuries, beginning around 1500 BC, though possibly a little earlier.

The home of the Aryans

The Khyber Pass, above Peshawar, in the Northwest Frontier of Pakistan. The road twists up into bare brown mountains, past rocky outcrops painted with the regimental honours of British army units who fought grim wars out here in Queen

Victoria's day. From the hilll overlooking the Afghan border at Torkham we can see queues of container lorries on the road between Pakistan and Kabul. Even up to the 1970s, these would still have been immense *kafilas* (camel caravans), 5 miles long, snaking down the pass twice a week – the drivers with their central Asian and Mongol faces, long plaited hair, gold teeth and brightly coloured clothes, and sporting old guns and daggers, children on their backs, their dogs as big as donkeys. The caravans brought kilims and bukhari rugs, jewels and precious stones from Badakshan, spices, medicines and herbs from the markets of Bukhara. It's been a crossing-place, a migration route, for thousands of years.

Looking from here across to the valley of the Kabul river, you can see the snow-capped ridges of the Hindu Kush, its ranges scored with the ancient passes that lead from central Asia down into India. It was from this region, the Rig-Veda says, that the Aryans spread eastwards into India from the fertile lands watered by the Kabul river, the Khurram, the Gomal and the Swat. From here, as it says in a later text, 'some went east … but some stayed at home in the west', among them the Gandhari tribe, who gave their name to the whole of what is now known as the

'Across many valleys, through rivers and gorges': the landscape of the Kabul river and the Hindu Kush mountains, scene of the earliest Aryan settlements in India.

Northwest Frontier. Archaeology, linguistics and genetics – plus common sense – are all consonant with the idea of a progressive migration of early Indo-European speakers taking place over several centuries. As we have seen, the world portrayed by the Rig-Vedic poets bears no recognizable relation to that of the Indus civilization; it has no memory of vast cities, except as ruins.

While the early poems of the Rig-Veda are set in the Punjab and eastern Afghanistan, the valleys of the Kabul river, the Swat and the Upper Indus, there are strong indications in those verses that this was not the Aryans' original homeland. They were aware that they had migrated from afar: that 'Indra had carried Yadu and Turvasa across the waters, crossing many rivers' going through 'narrow passes'. Remnants of these waves of migration are still traceable by linguists: most famous are the so-called Kaffirs of the Hindu Kush, the pagans of Chitral, descendants of Indo-Aryan peoples who, until the nineteenth century, spread over a much wider area of Afghan Nuristan. Encountered by Alexander the Great in about the fourth century BC, they still speak an archaic Indo-European language, and still worship an ancient 'Aryan' sky god called Di-Zau, who is cognate with the Greek Zeus (Dia) and the Sanskrit Dyaus-pitar. Traces of the migration thus survive to this day. But if their folk memory was that they had come from further west, where had the Aryans originated?

New discoveries in central Asia

Gonur Tepe, Turkmenistan. A howling gale has whipped up a sudden dust storm: grit swirls into our eyes and mouths as our jeep approaches an isolated archaeological site south of the Red Desert and the Aral Sea. We're a few hours along the old road from Askabad in the last days of Turkmanbashi, the idiosyncratic leader who took over this desert state after the fall of the Russian Empire. We have followed the old Silk Route across the plain north of the Elburz mountains to Mary, the ancient city of Merv in the Murghab oasis. Now a vast ruin field destroyed by the Mongols in the thirteenth century, the oasis had been a centre of civilization since prehistory. Finally, with sunset coming on, a low mound rises to the north: near it we see a mud-brick dig hut and a cluster of tents, flaps snapping in the wind. Under an awning Russian and Turkmen archaeologists are examining dramatic finds from a horse sacrifice buried around 1900 BC.

Victor Sarianidi is there to greet us. He can only be described as a living legend. Burly and charismatic, with a mane of white hair, his skin is burnt deep brown by the desert sun, and his voice rumbles like a camel clearing its throat. Sarianidi already has many great discoveries to his credit: it was he who dug up the amazing hoard of Bactrian gold at Tilya Tepe in northern Afghanistan. Great archaeologists have that unquantifiable gift, that nose for the right place to dig, and here he has hit gold again: a hitherto unknown civilization. Sarianidi had mapped more than 2000 Bronze Age sites in the area of the Murghab oasis, sites that seem to have suffered a dramatic collapse due to climate change in the same period as the decline of the Indus cities. Here, he thought, might be the biggest. Sure enough, out in the open desert, he found a huge defended area, plus a separate enclosed space that he interprets as a *temenos* (sacred enclosure).

The finds include not only horses and wheeled vehicles, but curved mud-brick fire altars – like elongated horseshoes – of the same shape and design as those still used in Vedic rites in India. Sunken bowls have also been found, containing traces of ingredients used for a sacred drink based on ephedra, a twiggy mountain plant believed to be the base ingredient of the Rig-Vedic *soma*. When infused in boiling water, ephedra produces quite a powerful sensation of euphoria (as I can testify). But here it's mixed with other ingredients – poppy seeds and cannabis – a fitting tipple for Indra!

The wind blows up in the late afternoon, lifting great swirling clouds of dust from the tractor blades that Sarianidi

BELOW

In camp in the Turkmen desert with the legendary Victor Sarianidi.

ભીમ   નકુળ   સહદેવ   અર્જુન   યુધિષ્ઠિર

The Mahabharata: *the greatest story ever told. Above: the Pandava brothers. Opposite: the battle of Kurukshetra. Told and retold over many centuries in all Indian languages, the* Mahabharata *became the story of India itself.*

adjacent forests since the Stone Age. The Rig-Veda shows that the Aryans burnt and cleared the forests for agricultural land, building forts with earth and timber ramparts. They used their surplus to enrich the warrior class and to uphold a basic three-tier division of society – priests, warriors and farmers. Below them the workers, servants and slaves came from the majority indigenous population. Here, perhaps, lies the root of the caste system. The divisions were apparently based on *varna* (colour) and *jati* (literally 'births', meaning the level of society or job you are born into). Very likely the colour of skin was used by the paler-skinned immigrants as a means of separation. Later, language and religious rites would become key definers. An inheritance from the Bronze Age, the caste system persists to this day; and even now, the majority of the underclass is descended from the aboriginal peoples.

This time of warfare may be distantly reflected in the most famous work of Indian literature, the *Mahabharata* – 'The Great Epic of India'. Just as Homer's *Iliad*, the tale of Troy, became a defining text of Greek culture, so the *Mahabharata* became the national epic of India, retold countless times and in many forms for over two millennia. For the orthodox Hindu, the war it describes is the dividing line between myth and reality: the beginning of political history.

The *Mahabharata* tells the tale of two clans, the Pandavas and the Kauravas, descended from the same grandfather, Kuru, head of a real clan that took his name and also appears in the Rig-Veda. It is a tale of war. Just as the *Iliad* begins with the wrath of Achilles 'that brought untold sufferings on the Greeks', so the *Mahabharata* starts with a fateful dissension, between the 'wrathful sons of Drita-rashtra, born of Kuru's royal kin … god-born men of god-like race'. The tale tells of a disputed succession of a kind that runs right through Indian history. In the end there is a terrible war and the final victory of the good, but, as at Troy, almost all the heroes on both sides die.

The location of the tale is the same as in the later historical poems of the Rig-Veda – on the river Jumna, centring on the region of Kurukshetra, the 'homestead of the Kurus'. Out of this comes the first defining myth of India, a great sprawling compendium of myths and morals. As a later commentator put it, 'what is here is nowhere else; what is not here is nowhere'. Indian audiences have loved it, admired its characters and referred to its dilemmas and moral judgements as exemplars for action for over two millennia, especially the key idea of dharma – the necessity of doing your duty.

The text as it stands amounts to roughly 100,000 verses – the longest poem in the world – and it probably reached its present shape between the last century BC and the first century AD. But its roots lie in bardic poetry of a much earlier epoch: the Sanskrit of the poem still carries traces of formulas of earlier Indo-European poetry. If we could see the version known to the grammarian Panini in the fifth century BC (only a fifth of its present length), we would no doubt be struck by the similarities to Homer's writings and other Iron Age heroic poetry. A Greek writer in the early second century AD refers to the Indians having 'an Iliad of 100,000 verses', which strongly suggests the text we have today. But the story was still expanding as late as the Gupta period (*c*. AD 320–600) because it mentions the Romans, the Hellenistic city of Antioch, and even the Huns' invasion of India in the fifth century AD.

The 'original' *Mahabharata*, then, was not unlike the *Iliad*, an Iron Age poem with fossilized verse forms from an even earlier time. But in the twentieth century the tale was put on a different footing by archaeological discoveries in the Ganges plain. After the archaeologist Heinrich Schliemann and his successors at Troy, Mycenae and Knossos brought the Greek heroic age to life, Indian archaeologists attempted to uncover a real Indian heroic age, and they began at the place in the story where the Kuru brothers ruled by the Ganges, 'in the royal hall of Hastinapur'.

Separating fact from fiction

We are driving across the cow belt, the Ganges plain, the heartland of Indian civilization, heading from Meerut 50 miles northeast of Delhi towards what is now the village of Hastinapur, the focus of the *Mahabharata*. All around us are green fields as far as the eye can see. The Ganges plain is one of the most fertile places on Earth, and has consequently attracted many people: the population of Uttar Pradesh and Bihar-Jharkand alone is more than that of the USA. Great tracts of this land were cleared for cultivation in the first millennium BC by 'Aryan' settlers from the northwest, led (so the Rig-Veda says) by Agni, the god of fire.

It is 'cow dust hour', the time before sunset when the bullock carts are heading back to the village, and dust churned up by their wheels rises into the warm air and golden light. Soon we enter the village, passing huge hostels for pilgrims, mainly of the Jain religion, who claim the site as the birthplace of two of their prehistoric founders. Presently a hill comes into view behind modern temples: this is the mound of the royal citadel, which in legend was the Troy of India, the residence of the Kauravas, and the place that sparked the fateful war that sealed the end of the heroic age when gods and heroes walked the Earth. But is there historical basis to the story? In India the *Mahabharata* has always been believed to be 'what happened', but colonial-period scholarship was both dismissive of the epic's literary merits and sceptical of any historical basis. Soon after Independence a young Indian archaeologist, B.B. Lal, set out to see if there was more to it. Before leaving for Hastinapur, I visited Lal in Delhi. Although now in his eighties, he is still hale and hearty, with a winning sense of humour and a still formidable command of detail.

Over the years he has been involved in many controversies surrounding early Indian history and archaeology. In his house he showed me black-and-whites slides he had taken in rural India a year or two after Independence – images that now seem almost like ancient history, nearer to the world of the epic than the neon-lit streets of modern Meerut. 'Well, you see the question that was worrying me most of the time was the historicity of the *Mahabharata* because there are two divergent views. According to one, everything in the text is true. According to the other, everything is imaginary. My approach was simply as an archaeologist.'

Fittingly, his was the first great dig by Indian archaeologists in newly independent India. In any state, even a modern democracy, it is crucial to establish a shared past, and the *Mahabharata* had been a crucial part of the Indian peoples' idea of a shared past over many centuries. Historiography, in a modern sense, had been established by the colonial power, the British. But epics such as the *Mahabharata* and *Ramayana* harked back to an older tradition, what one might call the dominant national culture in northern India, through folk plays, poems, songs and stories. To test the historicity of the national epic, Lal set out to examine sites mentioned in the *Mahabharata* on the same principle as Schliemann, Wilhelm Dorpfeld and Arthur Evans had uncovered the Greek Bronze Age. However exaggerated later by the bards, did the epic recall real places and even real events?

Lal went to Hastinapur in the autumn of 1949. The ancient city, named in Jain and Buddhist texts as the capital of the Kurus, had lain on the Ganges, which is now 3 miles away. The northern face of the mound still falls steeply 60 feet into the green farm fields, where a sluggish perennial stream is still known to local farmers as 'the old Ganges'. On the edge of the mound was a shrine to Shiva, 'Lord of the Pandavas', by the look of it not old, but a pointer to the tale that still haunted the local folk memory. Although the river was long gone, one of the old ghats (landing places) that once lay on it was still called after the epic's heroine Draupadi. Taking all this in, Lal scouted around for pottery finds in rain-eroded gulleys at the foot of the mound and soon turned up some distinctive thin, grey ware, often patterned with geometric designs filled with dots. 'It was *thali* plates and bowls, ordinary tableware, just as we use today,' Lal told me, 'and we immediately began to suspect it was prehistoric, a marker of north Indian Iron Age culture. So we came back in 1950 for three seasons. We stayed in tents, though the local Jain community let us use their kitchens. We used bullock carts to move the tools and lifting gear. We decided to put a great trench through the mound where we had found all the grey pottery in rain gulleys.'

The grey pottery proved crucial in dating the site. The citadel had lasted, Lal thought, till about 800 BC, when it was abandoned. Later genealogies, preserved in texts known as Puranas, described the abandonment of Hastinapur and the

movement of the rulers to Kausambi, lower down the Jumna, after a great flood. Remembering this story, Lal had an incredibly satisfying 'eureka' moment in the middle of the night, when he went down with an oil lamp to inspect the exposed site and saw that the Iron Age occupation had indeed been ended by a flood. 'There's nothing like that for an archaeologist,' Lal beamed. 'You feel very excited and you think, "Yes, I've got it"!'

None of this, of course, proved that the events of the *Mahabharata* war actually happened, or that its characters were real, but it proved that the bards who composed the earlier layers of the story in the Iron Age were writing about royal centres and clans that were important in the early part of that period: the setting of the story was back in the early first millennium BC.

Emboldened, Lal searched on. He and his colleagues took a look at over thirty other sites mentioned in the *Mahabharata,* all of which produced the same grey pottery. They also looked at the traditional site of the climactic battle at Kurukshetra in a tract of land north of Delhi, which has been the scene of several

ABOVE

Krishna and Balarama from an 18th-century manuscript. Krishna's advice to the warrior Arjuna on duty before the final battle became a key text of the 'right way' in Indian society. Even the secularist Nehru had a well-thumbed copy by his bedside.

great battles in Indian history. This is the *dharmaksetra* (holy field), the centre of the land where the battle is believed to have taken place, and where the god Krishna, disguised as a charioteer, revealed himself to the hero Arjuna before battle commenced, and spoke the famous words of wisdom, the *Bhagavadgita*, a text beloved of all Indians. Again from the pottery, Lal and his team identified an early Iron Age settlement out in the farmland half a mile beyond the medieval city, on a mound occupied by a village and topped with an old and revered Shiva temple.

Tonight is Sivaratri, the 'great night of Shiva', when visiting Kurukshetra is deemed especially auspicious. It's the February full moon, and all day crowds have been streaming from the city down the little country lanes lined with stalls selling pilgrim trinkets and souvenirs, food, and glasses of thick green *bhang* (cannabis), which adds an anarchic edge to the night of the great anarchist god himself. I walk past hostels for sadhus (holy men), retirement homes for old or invalid cows, to the Shiva temple and its bathing tank, festooned with strings of fairy lights. Unlike Hastinapur, this is only a small place, but perhaps realistically sized for a fortified farmstead of an Iron Age royal clan. Maybe this was the site of the real *kshetra* of the Kurus: a royal hall on a royal estate with earthen defences in waving wheatfields by the Jumna.

Lal had not proved that the story was true, but, like Schliemann at Troy and Mycenae, he had shown that the bardic tradition had handed down the names of real places that had existed at a particular time, and that later generations had preserved the names of those places. But what exactly had they remembered? An epic tale or a real event? Or an imaginative mixture of both? The Puranas suggested that a ninth-century date might be appropriate for the war, provided the genealogies had preserved the lineage of real people. Beyond the shadowy data of walls, pottery and 'tradition', Lal was prepared to discern the shadowy lineaments of ancient battles. On the basis of his painted grey ware, he suggested a date for the *Mahbharata* battle of around 860 BC. No more than with Troy, though, can we say that it really took place, but with India's extraordinary tenacity of folk memory, it would be unwise perhaps to dismiss the possibility out of hand.

Identity: a distillation of the past

The sun is setting as we head back to our hotel in Meerut (the town where the Great Indian Mutiny or, as Indians call it, the First War of Independence, began). We eat our meal looking over a packed bazaar, where crowds are out celebrating the festival. When he hears where we have been, our hotelier tells us a Meerut folk tale. Back in the fourteenth century, he says, Tamburlaine's army had invaded India, and the Mongol cavalry swept across the Ganges-Jumna doab, looting, burning and killing, a seemingly unstoppable force. But here in Meerut a heroic resistance was organized by a local scholar and poet, who called on the people to 'remember what Krishna said to Arjuna, and fight even though the odds against them seemed to be hopeless'. Organizing themselves into guerrilla forces that included women and children, they moved through the forests, braving the most brutal reprisals and harassing the invaders 'to defend the people and land of Bharat', until eventually the harried and baffled Mongols withdrew.

Mulling over the hotelier's tale, while Sivaratri fireworks go off in the street like volleys of gunfire, another thought comes to me about the *Mahabharata*. It describes a past that may seem to be timeless, always there, tempting some to see India as a place of thought and inaction. But the reverse is true: the nation was born of struggle. The ancient commentators referred to the epic as *sruti*, which means 'what actually happened'. That intuition is right. It tells of the 'real' world, of war and destruction, violence and betrayal, the vanity of ambition, the futility of anger and hatred. Its heroes have feet of clay, but ultimately good triumphs even in a time of cosmic destruction. The epic then is one of action, and behind all the accretions at its core is a realistic view of the tragedies of history: good men on either side suffer and die; time moves on and the cities of the epic are swept away by the Ganges. New capitals are built. The wounds of history heal in time. Over the next 3000 years Greeks and Kushans, Turks and Afghans, Mughals and British, Alexander, Tamburlaine and Babur, will all come and fall under India's spell. And India's greatest strength, one known only to the oldest civilizations, will be to adapt and change, to use the gifts of history and to accept its wounds, but somehow, magically, to be always India.

2
The Power of Ideas

DAYBREAK IN BENARES. The end of the night is heralded by the sound of birds on my window sill. A pale wash of light touches the crumbling façades of the maharajas' palaces and the prancing tigers on the house of the Dom Raja, the keeper of the funeral pyres. Swathed in blankets against the chill air, knots of pilgrims file down to the water's edge to strip off and plunge in. Gasping at the coldness and holding a handful of water with outstretched arms

towards the first pink hint of the sun, they recite the ancient mantra: 'Giver of life, remover of pain and sorrow, bestower of happiness, creator of the universe, may we receive your supreme, sin-destroying light; may you guide our minds towards good …'

I have come here many times over the years, but familiarity has never dulled the sheer thrill of this scene. For all the ravages of modernity, the crumbling infrastructure and the pollution of Mother Ganges, Benares is still a beautiful city, one of the most evocative on Earth. It is a city of the imagination, which never fails to fulfil its promise of mystery and enchantment. All too often the technological brilliance of the global age of mass communication kills the past and breaks these older allegiances in just a few generations. But not here. In Benares are 2500 years of stories, of life lived in the city's narrow lanes. The Banarsis have their shrines, their music, their customs and dialect, their funeral pyres, their thick, bitter curd cooling in the alleys in handmade earthenware bowls, their jugs of sour green *bhang* for the nights of Shiva the transgressor, the god of excess – invisible topographies ingrained in the minds of those lucky enough to be born inside the old city.

The lodging house teeters on a steeply stepped bathing ghat. From the rooftop the magnificent frontage of the city stretches 3 miles on a great curve of the river, the sun rising downstream across wide sandbanks and jungle, where in heavy monsoons the flood can spread to the horizon. As the sun comes up over the trees, it gilds the water, where skiffs with long oars float along the glittering surface like water-flies on a path of gold. Below me, through the branches of the old pipal tree at our front door, a lady in a yellow sari sprinkles petals of jasmine on a *linga*m (the phallic stone of Shiva) at the foot of the trunk, and pours Ganges water on the vermilioned stones among its tangled roots. In the alley, boys are heading to Vedic school, the master of the wrestling school rakes his sandpit, and the pandits set up their tattered umbrellas and well-fingered almanacs to receive the day's clients. This is a great Hindu city in a time of Hindu revival. But things were once very different.

The story of India brings us now to the fifth century BC, the time when Greek civilization was the powerhouse of the eastern Mediterranean. At that time the Persians ruled the greatest empire on Earth. Darius the Great had conquered the lands from the Aegean to the Indus, and brought the early Indian kingdoms in the Punjab and the Ganges and Jumna valleys into contact with the dazzling imperial kingship of their distant linguistic and cultural cousins. Benares, the place where the Buddha preached his first sermon, was then simply the capital of one small northern Indian kingdom. This was a time when Hinduism as we know it today, with the cults and gods we see in every corner of the city, didn't exist. Although the pandits tell the visitor myths of the city's primordial antiquity (and in India myth has an uncanny way of creating its own reality), the archaeologists tell us that the first urban settlement on the site of Benares began only in the sixth century BC, at what is now known as Rajghat (the king's riverbank), the crossing point of the great historical route that later became the Grand Trunk Road, which today is carried over the river by the Curzon railway bridge. There were brick buildings, perhaps fortified with brick defences, and a clay embankment against the river floods. But the place rapidly expanded in the fifth century to become a centre for long-distance trade and textile production, as it has been ever since. We have no real evidence for its size, but the city of Kausambi, from the same era, has been excavated and had massive revetted, burnt-brick defences, with a 6-mile circuit, all of which suggests a booming population with powerful authorities able to deploy large-scale communal labour. It was this new urban civilization that was the setting for the next stage of the story of India.

The Axis age

The achievements of the great civilizations encompass the whole range of human creativity, from the practical and the artistic to the intellectual and spiritual. And nowhere has this been truer than in India. The pursuit of knowledge has had an almost religious value in Indian civilization, and still does today, even in India's headlong rush into modernity. The formative time happened in the few generations either side of 500 BC. This has become known as the Axis age because so many of the great thinkers of the Old World lived at this same moment: the Buddha and Mahavira in India; Confucius, Lao Tzu and Chuang Tzu in China; the Old Testament prophets; the Greek philosophers; even, it has been suggested, Zoroaster. This idea has recently met with criticism. That Lao Tzu ever existed is a moot point, while Zoroaster clearly is to be dated many centuries earlier among the herders of central Asia. And whether it is valid at all to suggest a relationship between these great developments in the history of ideas has been questioned. Nevertheless, the insight, I think, is useful and broadly true, in the sense that in the Middle Iron Age the old, ritualistic ideas of religion inherited by the ancient civilizations from the Bronze Age were all essentially expressions of the ideology of the rulers. As such, they were subject to profound questioning in urban societies, where the old social order was changing and new mercantile classes were on the rise. Obviously, this was true in several places across Eurasia, certainly in the mixed cultures of the Levant, and in Iron Age Greece where the 'orientalizing revolution' from the Near East transformed Hellenic culture.

Here in the Ganges plain, in the fifth century BC, new cities were developing and trade routes were opening up across the world. Perhaps this was accelerated by the existence of the Persian Empire, whose official language shared a common root with Sanskrit. (In fact, all through the history of India the close relation of the Indian and Persian languages is a factor in the exchange of ideas between the subcontinent, central Asia and the Iranian plateau.) At this time there were many thinkers in different fields – astronomy, geometry, grammar, linguistics and phonetics (indeed, in the third century BC writing would be reintroduced to India for the first time since the unknown writing system of Indus cities). But this was also a time of speculation about the nature of the human condition itself.

Rethinking the world

Since the time of the Rig-Veda, and no doubt long before, Indians had meditated on the nature of the universe and the place of human beings within it. This fundamental obsession was compounded in the fifth century BC by a growing questioning of the moral and social order promulgated by the Brahmin priests in a rigid caste system. What was the meaning of life and what part did humanity play in the chain of being? On whose authority existed the power systems that controlled peoples' lives even beyond birth and death? The Vedic belief in the cycle of life, with its belief in karma and rebirth, had the effect of fixing the poor in poverty, and the rich above them, the pattern being repeated through their children and their children's children. India is still battling with this legacy today. Subject to horrendous discrimination and violence even now, the untouchables and lower castes have only recently found a voice in India's post-Independence democracy, although the debate began many centuries earlier.

In the fifth century BC seekers after truth in the cities of the Ganges plain were as varied and numerous as their contemporaries in the pre-Socratic societies of Greece and the Ionian islands. There were sceptics, rationalists, atheists and determinists. There were those who rejected any idea of an afterlife, and those who proposed that the world is composed of atoms, as did their contemporary, Heraclitus of Ephesus, who believed 'all is change'. There were others who thought all change was illusory and held that the universe is bound together by immutable laws. But there were also those who denied the gods altogether and rejected the Brahminical order.

Among the most important and long-lasting seekers after truth were the Jains, who have had a profound influence on Indian thought and society for more than 2000 years. They have always drawn support from the trading communities, especially in Gujarat in western India, one of the main centres of the Bronze Age

Indus civilization. Their chief leader Mahavira, 'the great soul', was an historical character, a contemporary of the Buddha, who in Jain tradition came at the end of a long line of gurus. Although the religion emerged in the fifth century BC, it probably had much more ancient roots. Some Jain ideas, especially the principle of *ahimsa* (non-harm or non-violence) to all living things, even insects, sound very archaic indeed. (Could they even be prehistoric?) The sect still survives today, and the notion of *ahimsa* is one of the great ideas of Indian culture, percolating right down to Mahatma Gandhi and the freedom movement.

However, the most influential of these early groups, not only in India but the world, were those who followed a teacher whom we know as the Buddha. He was a prince from a land-owning family, whose clan were rulers in the Nepali *terai*, the steamy borderland between India and the foothills of the Himalayas. His ideas spread beyond India to China, Korea, Japan and the whole of eastern Asia, also to Afghanistan and central Asia, the wisdom of India seducing East and West. This phase of India's history, then, is a fascinating story of great empires and giant figures, but it is above all about the power of ideas.

Buddhism: an end to suffering

It is 2 a.m. From Gaya Station we make our way to the Hotel Classic, where we are offered puri and vegetables with hot sweet tea, welcome after the long hours on a delayed train down from Benares. The morning papers are full of the bombings that have taken place in Benares, both at the station and the Hanuman temple. It is a reminder that no society in history has been immune to violence; and for all its great tradition of non-violence, India is no exception. Indeed, India's history has been uniquely violent, and one might think that it is precisely because of this that India has meditated so long and hard about the causes of violence and the need to restrain it. Violence has continued to be a part of the subcontinent's experience since Independence, as evidenced by the wars with Pakistan, the Bangladesh conflict and the war in Kashmir. All are part of the continuing aftermath of the 1947 Partition which took place on the grounds of religion. These events continue to give fuel to the sectarians, hence the demolition of a mosque in Ayodhia in 1992, one of the most charged events in Indian history since Partition, which has spawned further conflict, such as that in 2001 in Gujarat. The world of the Buddha was very different from ours. But like a therapist, the Buddha is diagnosing the condition of the human mind, and that, I daresay, has not changed. We underestimate the people of the past at our peril.

Outside the station approaches, Buddhist pilgrims are heading in rickshaws on the short trip to Bodhgaya, the place where the Buddha found enlightenment.

LEFT

The miraculous birth of the Buddha from an 18th-century Burmese manuscript. The transformation of the Buddha's tale with fairytale elements really began under Kushans in the 1st and 2nd centuries AD when the story expanded along the Silk Route to China and east Asia.

OPPOSITE

The giant Buddha at Bodhgaya today: the Master himself would have thoroughly disapproved of his deification.

The journey takes us through green fields alongside the Phalgu river, dried up at this time of year: it is a yellow expanse of windblown sand, edged by jungle and backed by distant wooded hills. The Buddha walked across it from the little homestead where he is supposed to have broken his fasting and austerities to take porridge from a woman whose name the tradition remembers as Sujata. This was to be the last step before his moment of destiny.

The young man had been a prince of an old *kshatriya* (warrior caste) landowning clan, the Sakyamunis, who came from the foothills on the edge of Nepal. But he was a prince who renounced that life and all its privileges. His reasons for going were said to be four. He saw the reality of the human condition in the spectacle of disease, illness, suffering and death after witnessing an old man, a blind

man, a dying man and then a corpse. (These are sights you can still see any day on the streets of India.) The prince left his home and all the pleasures of his rank to seek an answer: an end to suffering He turned his back on the most human intimacies, his loving wife and their helpless child, in order to discover his humanity. A paradox? The Buddha's life is full of paradoxes. Since his time there have sprung up so many myths about him, so many miraculous tales, that it is hard to get back to the man himself and what he actually preached. But that depends on the context. He was arguing with other sects, especially the Brahmins. He was contesting their ritualized vision of the universe and their predetermined conception of human society. His ideas formed a reaction, then, a questioning of the old order. He was a protestor.

So when he lived matters, but, unfortunately, it is not even certain what century that was. Tradition says that he died around a date equivalent to 486 BC in the Western calendar, but recently there has been a growing feeling that the date should be brought down to the fourth century, making him almost a contemporary of Alexander the Great. The controversy centres on the nature of the society in the Ganges plain as depicted in Buddhist texts, all of which were written down much later than his time. These texts assume a backdrop of urban societies, not villages but cities, where the mercantile classes in particular found his message of trust and 'right conduct' congenial. On his travels the Buddha is described as visiting bustling cities, many of which – if they existed at all – must have been new in the fifth century. Another perplexing fact is the apparent silence on Buddhism for more than two centuries after his death, until the accession of the emperor Ashoka in *c*.270 BC. Did Buddhism stand still, remaining an insignificant cult until it was picked up by the emperor and turned into something like an 'official' ideology? This has led many scholars to argue a fourth century BC date, though it may well be that Buddhism stayed a small cult until it was taken up by the emperor (a distant parallel might be Constantine's adoption of Christianity).

As for the cities, some of those excavated, such as Kausambi with its huge perimeter defences, were certainly in existence by the sixth century. So there is still much to be said for the traditional dating. Crucial supporting evidence is the traditional chronology recorded in Pali chronicles in Sri Lanka from the fourth to the sixth centuries AD, which are based on historical material going back to the time

of the emperor Chandragupta Maurya (*c.*320–293 BC), two generations before Ashoka. These converge with remarkable precision on the traditional date. So while the eighty years traditionally allotted to the Buddha's life is a suspiciously round figure (did he really spend forty-five years wandering around rural Bihar and northern India?), a fifth-century date for his death, and even a death date of 485/6, is still possible.

On the road to enlightenment

So Prince Siddhartha (as he was) left his family to live the life of an Indian ascetic, mortifying his body. You still meet such people on the road – these days even with their mobile phones – gathering at the annual *melas* (festivals), starving themselves, practising austerities, holding an arm in the air, standing on one leg and keeping a

ABOVE

The legend of the Buddha descending from heaven (after visiting his dead mother) at Sankasya, now a small place in Uttar Pradesh. The event was later com- mememorated by the emperor Ashoka.

RIGHT AND BELOW

The stupa at Sarnath outside Benares (right), marks the site of the Buddha's first sermon and his last words (below), shown in the death scene at Kushinagar in this Tibetan painting.

dysentery after eating pork (like most ancient Indians, the Buddha was not vegetarian). He knew he was about to die. None of his utterances was recorded at any point near his own time; when there was no writing. They were set down in Pali four centuries later. But there is an utterly convincing realism in the old man's urgent, exasperated response as his disciples – devastated at the prospect of losing him – continue to ask for his guidance: 'What about the *sangam*, the community?' He had, after all, always told them that his teaching was only like a boat or a raft, to get across the river: 'Once you get to the other side, you don't try to pick the boat up and carry on walking with it; you leave it by the water and push on.'

His life ebbing away, he said: 'What do you expect of me? I have taught the truth. I have held nothing back … You are the community now. Be a lamp to yourselves. Be your own refuge. Seek for no other.' His final words were these: 'All things must pass. Strive on. Don't give up.'

In hindsight, the Buddha was not setting out to found a new religion – indeed, one may well question whether that's what Buddhism actually is. Certainly, it is not a religion in the way that the devotees of Christianity and Islam regard their beliefs. Nor was he claiming to be divine. He was adamant with his followers that they should not deify him. Buddhism might have remained a local teaching, one of many in the Ganges plain that arose from the thinkers of the fifth century, many of whom knew each other, crossed paths and debated together. Among these were the Jains, who still survive as an Indian phenomenon and have had a profound influence on Indian civilization.

Today we see the Buddha's message as so compelling, and its worldwide influence as being so great, that its historical trajectory was inevitable, but Buddhism could have faded away like other Axis age cults, such as Ajivikism. We know his teachings were assembled soon after his death by his immediate followers, at a council held at Rajgir. But it was as much as 200 years later that the message began to go out to a wider world. At that time this regional sect was taken up as an official ideology by a powerful local dynasty that had turned itself into the first empire of India. So the next phase of the story is tied up with great historical events. And the catalyst, as so often in history, was war.

Alexander the Great and the coming of the Greeks

Back in 500 BC – perhaps during the Buddha's lifetime – the Persian king Darius the Great invaded the Indus region and exacted tribute from its peoples. On his inscriptions the people of Gandhara (around Peshawar in Pakistan) are listed among his subject peoples, and on the walls of the great palace at Persepolis the ambassadors of 'Hindush' (the Indus valley) are shown paying tribute with (among other things) what look like bales of fine Indian textiles. The Persian attempt to go west ended with their decisive defeat by the Greeks in 480 BC. The Greeks, however, never forgot the Persian desecration of their temples, and in 334 BC Alexander the Great invaded Asia in a war of conquest and belated retribution. Indian elephants and soldiers were among the terrified ranks in the dust storm at Arbela in October 331 BC, when Alexander overcame the great king's army and destroyed the Persian monarchy. Four years later the Macedonians burst into the plains of India. In 327 BC the army crossed the Khyber Pass, bridged the Indus, and occupied the Indian city of Taxila in the Punjab. That May, as the monsoon rains fell, Alexander forced a crossing of the Jhehum river and won a savage battle against the local raja in the Punjab, whose name the Greeks report as Porus, perhaps one of the ancinet Aryan clan of the Purus. Fragments in later Greek sources show the reactions of Alexander's army to India – to its climate and monsoons, its flora and fauna. Greek botanists and philosophers offered the first observations on the country, even the connections between the languages (Greek is affiliated with the eastern Indo-European linguistic group, which includes Old Iranian and Sanskrit). It was the beginning of a long and fruitful interaction.

Believing India to be a narrow peninsula whose eastern borders bounded the shore of the 'Great Ocean', Alexander moved east through the Punjab during the monsoon season of 327. He crossed the Chenab and Ravi rivers in early September, and stopped at the Beas river in the pleasant countryside outside Amritsar. This was a strategic tract of land, where battles have been fought since the days of the Rig-Veda right up to the Sikh wars against the British. What intelligence the Greeks had about the road ahead is unclear, and they seem to have known that there were powerful kingdoms down the Ganges, but after a debate among the leadership, the weary army turned back. They fought bitter battles and sieges along the rivers south of today's Lahore, where the ancient cities around Harappa were sacked, but the Greeks suffered heavy losses, from fighting and sickness, and Alexander himself nearly died from his wounds. Eventually he made his exit from the Indus delta via the inhospitable wastes of the Makran desert. However the Greeks dressed it up, the Indian campaign ended in anticlimax. Despite his ambition to rule India and to see the ends of the Earth, Alexander never stepped on Indian soil again.

The first Indian empire

So Alexander came and saw, but India was not conquered. For all his glamour in Western history, Alexander is mentioned in no early Indian source. Nonetheless, the Greek–Indian contact would prove fantastically enriching. In culture and politics, particularly in the northwest, the synthesis would have a lasting impact. The world had opened up. His expedition, together with the political upheavals it set in motion between Iraq and the Indus, were to be the catalyst for the first great Indian empire. It was led by Chandragupta Maurya, one of the greatest leaders and organizers in Indian history. An adventurer from the land of Magadha, around Rajgir, the young Chandragupta – so the Greeks later reported – had met Alexander, and been inspired by his power, charisma and the glamour of his violence. The tale of his rise from nowhere, complete with divinely inspired omens, survives in Greek sources.

Having been driven into exile by the Nanda king in Maghada, Chandragupta led a revolt to expel the Greek garrisons from the Punjab, and after a series of battles, he overthrew the king himself and seized power in Maghada. This bitter warfare left grim memories in the Buddhist tradition of 'eighty corpse dances', of gibbets and impalings. Chandragupta then extended his power over northern India from the Indus to the Ganges. The Greek king Seleucus Nicator, Alexander's successor in the eastern Hellenistic empire, now moved against him with a great army, and fought in the Indus valley, but was unable to defeat him. By 302 BC Chandragupta found himself ruler of the first great Indian state – a state that can be fairly described as the first predecessor of today's India.

Wary, suspicious, masterful and surrounded by a personal guard of female warriors – Indian Amazons – Chandragupta understood the nature of power with a cool-eyed clarity, and ruthlessly deployed spies and assassins in a surveillance state. The chief surviving testimony to his rule is the famous *Arthashastra*. This is India's first great text on statecraft, which tradition says was composed by his wily chief minister Kautilya, who masterminded Chandragupta's triumph over the Nanda king. Although the text as we have it has many accretions (it proved useful to a number of later emperors), that tradition may well be true. Written long before Machiavelli, the book's psychological insight into human nature and its weak points has impressed all who encounter it, and is even now used as a model by modern Indian business schools and military analysts.

The central idea of the work is the *artha* (prosperity) of a kingdom – how to get it and how to keep it. Kautilya advocates the application of agents, surveillance and diplomacy beyond the frontiers to ensure the maintenance of power ('My enemy's enemy is my friend' is one of the *Arthashastra*'s many memorable sayings). The state is not seen as a moral order, but

BELOW

The tale of Chandragupta in the famous Amar Chitra Katha series of comic books.

purely as a system of power relations defined by the limits of what is practically feasible. At the centre is the king, whose natural enemies are his immediate neighbours; his enemies' further neighbours are his natural friends. The ruler's ability to hold power, says Kautilya, depends on the seven pillars of power. These were: the king's personal quality and that of his ministers, the wealth of his provinces and of his chief city, his treasury, his army and, last but not least, the success of his diplomacy in the cultivation of allies. In all this Chandragupta proved as adept as any ruler in history.

Around the year 300 BC Chandragupta cemented his power by diplomatic exchanges with Seleucus Nicator. This provided him with 300 war elephants ('and certain powerful aphrodisiacs'!) in exchange for an agreement defining India's 'natural frontier' – a goal sought after by all imperialists in India, right down to the British. India would now be bounded by the Hindu Kush, the Afghan mountains and the Baluchi desert. As part of the deal, he married a Greek princess, so his grandson Ashoka, perhaps the greatest ruler in Indian history, may have had Greek blood, and perhaps even spoke a little of the language.

It was in the aftermath of these events that the first Westerners, so far as we know, reached the heart of India. In about 302 BC a Greek embassy, led by ambassador Megasthenes, visited the Ganges plain. Megasthenes wrote a book about his time in India, which is now lost, but it survives in fragments quoted by other writers. It is the first foreign description of India, and the first datable account of its social order, customs, caste system and kingship. Its anecdotes provide a fascinating window on the world of early India.

After their long journey from Babylon, the Greeks made their way through the Khyber Pass and down the old highway across the Punjab from Taxila (the ancestor of the Grand Trunk Road). En route they passed Alexander's altars on the Beas river, where a Greek source, Plutarch, says Chandragupta was later accustomed to do puja, a prayer ritual, in memory of the Macedonian king. Then they made their way by boat down the Jumna and the Ganges past the cities of Kausambi and Benares, no doubt remarking, as all later travellers would, on the fertility and beauty of the countryside. Surviving fragments of Megasthenes' book give us a vivid sense of the Greeks' open-mouthed entry into an alien world that Alexander had only ever encountered at its fringes, and then with violence. Sailing down the Ganges, they saw at first hand 'the greatest river in India, worshipped by all Indians, which is all of a hundred stadia [11 miles] wide, sometimes so that one cannot see the far shore'.

At last they came in sight of Chandragupta's capital, Pataliputra, today's Patna, in Bihar. This bustling city of 1.5 million inhabitants is seldom mentioned these days on the tourist trail, but it is one of most important and interesting places in Indian history. Founded in the sixth century BC, it would be the chief city of northern India until the Gupta age in the fourth century AD, and through all the later phases of its life down to the Mughals, the East India Company and the freedom movement. It is a living witness to the drama of Indian history.

Patna: India's first imperial city

We sail at dawn with a Patna boatman from Collectors Ghat, the upstream landing place where the British built their offices, villas and opium warehouses from the eighteenth century onwards. Floating slowly downstream, as the Greeks did so long ago, we pass early morning bathers and head straight into the rising sun – for the Ganges flows almost due east as it passes the city. Viewed from the river, Patna is still low-rise, with woods, gardens and clumps of palms. The shore is dotted with gaily painted shrines, both Hindu and Muslim. During the Middle Ages Patna became a noted centre of Islam, and can boast over a dozen important *darghas* (tombs) of Sufi saints, their white onion domes dotting the riverbank. Soon the boat is drifting past immense ruined palaces, medieval Mughal fortresses, drum towers keeling over into the water, their huge walls displaced by the relentless flow of the river, their crumbling bastions silted with thick mud the colour of chocolate. As the sun rises above the city, it is as if we are sailing in slow motion past an Indian Rome.

Gradually, the silting of the river pulls the channel away from the line of the old walls, and the boat drifts alongside a great shoulder of whitened sand about 20 feet above the water. On the shore between the city and the river are a dozen

LEFT

Dawn at Patna. Sailing down the Ganges reveals a spectacular panorama of ruined fortresses, palaces and shrines.

Street in Patna in c. 1825, by which time the city had contracted within its medieval defences to a third of its ancient size; it was still estimated by the British surveyor Francis Buchanan as having 300,000 people.

towering brick-kiln chimneys rearing up one after the other, some with long smudges of smoke hanging in the dawn air. The whole scene begins to take on the feel of a dystopian fantasy in science fiction. At the landing place are three big wooden sand barges with giant skeletal stern rudders and huge lateen sails, their torn and patched grey canvas hanging limp in the still air. Beside them women are cooking at a fire, while others in bright saris are bathing and laughing. We pull in under long, bending bamboo poles with snapping flags, and scamper up the bank past the shrines of Shiva and the monkey god Hanuman under a spreading tree. From the riverbank it's a 100-yard walk through a brickyard with towering chimneys up to what was once the medieval waterfront, which crowns a steep rise lined with red-brick mansions and old shrines. The former landing place is now high and dry, crowned by a lovely Sufi shrine that once commanded beautiful vistas over the river. And so we enter the old Mughal and British town, the eastern end of the city that played such a role in Indian history for nearly ten centuries, and which, after Delhi, was India's greatest imperial city.

Buddhist tradition tells of the Master's prophecy that Patna would be the greatest of all centres of trade and population. In the first century BC the author of the text known as the Yuga Purana saw Mauryan Patna as the fruition of urban life in early India. He wrote: 'On the southern and most excellent bank of the Ganges the royal sage will cause a lovely city to be founded, filled with people and flower gardens. And that pleasant city will endure for 5000 years.'

Chandragupta Maurya's capital, so the Greeks recorded, stood at the junction of the Ganges and the Erranoboas (the latter derived from the ancient Sanskrit name for the river Son, Hiranyabahu, meaning 'golden armed'). The city stretched for nearly 10 miles along the Ganges, and was about $1\frac{1}{2}$ miles deep, making a circuit of 22 miles. According to Megasthenes, the city had sixty-four gates and 570 towers. These seem almost incredible figures, but remnants of stockades and tower bases found a century ago in the British period tend to confirm his story. Given the strength of the seasonal inundations, the defences were mainly wooden, consisting of huge palisades with piles sunk along the riverside to give better protection against the flooding of the Ganges. The main gates had wide, timber-floored walk-ways through the ramparts, with bridges across an outer ditch system fed by water from the Son, which was 600 feet wide on the landward side and fed a network of smaller canals. Inside the city were massive buildings of burnt brick, with stone and wooden columns, and decorated plaster. 'I have seen the great cities of the east,' wrote Megasthenes, 'I have seen the Persian palaces of Susa and Ecbatana, but this is the greatest city in the world.'

From a distance the townscape of gardens, trees, ornamental woodland, parks and menageries might have given the impression of a vast pleasure garden, rather like Kublai Khan's magic world of Xanadu, or the peony and cherry gardens of imperial Xian celebrated by the poets of the Tang dynasty in China. In other words, the Asiatic city might be seen as a royal ritual enclosure, and a far cry from today's bustling, proletarian Indian city. But on closer inspection – and Indian ministers and equerries plied them with mind-boggling facts (some no doubt exaggerated for effect) – the Greeks rapidly came to understand that Pataliputra was, in fact, a vast military base. Outside the walls to the south was an enormous cantonment of the kind later laid out by the British, a semi-permanent camp for the royal army, which, so the Greek visitors were informed, amounted to 40,000 men (out of a full military establishment claimed to number 400,000, with 3000 war elephants). As for the ruler's own residence, the palace area lay in a great oblong to the south, inside separate moated defences. There Chandragupta Maurya himself kept court, ever vigilant for insurrection, 'never sleeping by day', as Megasthenes reports, surrounded by his female bodyguard 'loyal only to him', yet still 'by night obliged to change his couch from time to time to thwart plots against his life'.

Portrait of early Indian society

Even in the fragments preserved in the pages of later historians, the Greeks' first view of India is one of those texts from history – like the letters of Cortes from Mexico – that tells us how it feels to encounter another world. 'There are one hundred and eighteen separate nations in India,' noted Megasthenes with amazement (and presumably his informants could speak only of the lands under Mauryan rule). No wonder the Greeks overwhelmed by the scale of it all, and by the sheer exoticism, which at times led them to descend to literally fabulous fairy tales. There were sections on climate, custom and even on the physiognomy of the Indians. There were lengthy digressions on elephant hunting and tigers, on cotton and banyan trees. The Greeks noted disapprovingly that the Indians did not make eating the social ritual that it was in the Mediterranean, where the communal meal was also a religious rite, as it still is today. 'The Indian people,' Megasthenes remarked, 'take food at any time of the day, and even singly if they wish.'

Like every modern visitor, Megasthenes noticed the Indians' 'love of adornment', especially gold jewellery and precious gems, and their 'brightly coloured cotton garments, a brighter colour than any other'. He adds, 'For since they esteem beauty so highly, they do everything they can to beautify their appearance.' But a cultural trait that particularly impressed the Greeks was the Indian respect for 'the superiority of wisdom above all', and their emphasis on simplicity, frugality, 'orderliness' and 'self-restraint' in daily life. Even more striking is his observation that 'No Indians ever set out beyond their own country to wage aggressive war because of their respect for justice'.

Coming from a literate society, the Greeks were surprised by 'the lack of written letters' in a memorizing society, where 'everything is regulated from memory'. Given that, one of the most surprising elements in Megasthenes' account is the level of organization Chandragupta achieved over such a wide empire. With government departments for the supervision of public works, roads, prices, markets and harbours, and with joint administration of military affairs, transport and naval supply, the degree to which memory and custom regulated Indian society is revealed in one of the most fascinating sections of Megasthenes' lost text, which gives the first outside account of the caste system:

> The population of India is divided into seven castes. The first is
> formed by the collective body of the philosophers [Brahmins].
> These in numbers are inferior to the rest, but in dignity are pre-
> eminent. They are exempt from public duties, but are engaged by
> private persons to perform the necessary rituals of life and death.

For they are believed to be most dear to the gods, and most conversant with matters pertaining to the world of the spirits. In requital of such services, they receive valuable gifts and privileges.

Elsewhere (as recorded by the geographer Strabo), Megasthenes talks about the Brahmins of the mountains worshipping Dionysus (Shiva?) and in the plains, especially around Mathura, worshipping Heracles (Krishna?). He also adds a fascinating and little-noticed reference to a huge annual gathering, 'the great assembly, as it is called'. This took place each year in January in northern India when 'all the philosophers [Brahmins and holy men] come together at the gates of the king', where they perform rituals and iron out issues of civil and religious law. Such a gathering, accompanied by a great royal distribution of alms, is described by the Chinese Buddhist pilgrim Hsuan Tsang in AD 640 as 'having gone on since ancient times' at Prayag, today's Allahabad, where great annual *melas* are still held, and where every twelve years the *Kumbh Mela* takes place, the largest gathering anywhere on Earth.

Megasthenes also describes the other ranks of Indian society. He writes of the peasant cultivators, who formed the mass of the population, and 'who pay a land tax and a fourth of their yield', the cattle herders and shepherds, the hunters, trappers and bird-catchers, and the artisans, craftsmen, wood- and metal-workers. The fifth caste in his scheme is the military (*kshatriyas*), a numerous class, who lived at leisure in time of peace. They were 'well organized and equipped for war, with a huge establishment of elephants and war horses'. Megasthenes also tells us that there was a royal fleet, with shipbuilders and a 'first sea lord' who let out ships for commercial purposes in time of peace. Going outside the customary fourfold division of castes we find in early Indian texts, he assigns a separate category to the civil service (*ephors*), 'whose duty is to enquire into and report everything that goes on in India to the royal government or magistrates'. Similarly, he makes a seventh caste, the smallest in numbers, of councillors, administrators, governors, judges, army commanders and chief magistrates. Megasthenes concludes by noting caste rules – 'no one is allowed to marry outside his caste, or exercise any calling but his own: a soldier cannot become a peasant; an artisan cannot become a [Brahmin] philosopher.'

Megasthenes' fascinating account is the first of Indian society and the caste system to be written by an outsider. It is interesting that he expands the basic four castes of the ancient texts – Brahmins, warriors, traders and farmers – to a sevenfold division, which is in fact found in southern Indian Brahminical accounts of the caste system, though no doubt then, as now, there were thousands of subcastes. Essentially, though, he corroborates the information in the *Arthashastra*, which is

ascribed in its earliest form to the time of Chandragupta. He also mentions what are clearly Stone Age indigenous tribes in a number of areas, with whom the Mauryans had contact, among them 'wild people' living in the Himalayas around the source of the Ganges. Many such peoples survive today. The one section of society he may not have come into contact with as a foreigner (though its members are mentioned in the *Arthashastra*) was the *chandalas* (untouchables). These lived outside towns and were viewed as polluted, so they were forbidden, for example, from using the wells of other castes. How this form of oppression arose is still disputed, but it has been sustained over millennia and is still very strong, despite India's democratic constitution and the further legislation on untouchability since the 1980s which has sought to abolish it. In general, caste rules were not as rigid as Megasthenes makes them sound, and medieval Muslim and later British observers were equally misled by the possibilities of diversification within the castes and movement between them. But the core principles of caste are still functioning, as can be seen from any marriage column today in India's Sunday newspapers.

The legend of Chandragupta

Of the physical remains of the city of Chandragupta there are few traces. The broad topography is still there, with the Ganges , 5 miles wide in the rainy seasons, defining the northern edge of the city. The Son river has shifted and now meets the Ganges 20 miles upstream. For such an important site, there has been very little excavation. Indeed, it was only a century or so ago that British archaeologist Laurence Waddell, with growing excitement, was able to prove that the physical remains of ancient Pataliputra lay underneath the modern city. Even the wooden walls described by Megasthenes were exposed. They were made of sal tree trunks, their tops 20 feet below the present ground level, and the remains of the great moat described by Megasthenes, an old channel of the river Son, also still existed. It was 200 yards wide and still known in one place as Maharaj Khanda, 'the emperor's moat'.

But of Chandragupta himself there is one specific and remarkable survival. This is at the Kamaldah Jain temples, which lie on a picturesque wooded peninsula inside the city. They are set in a beautiful lake, the 'lotus pond', where fishermen still cast their nets from boats only a few hundred yards from the railway track. The lake shore, with its fruit orchards, is now being encroached on by Patna's burgeoning urban sprawl, but here it is still possible to imagine the city of pools and pleasure gardens described by the Greeks. The main shrine stands on a deep mound of ancient debris, its crumbling brick plinth surrounded by trees. You climb a flight of steps on to a sun-baked plastered platform with a little sanctum on top. According to the custodian, it commemorates not one of the twenty-four Jain

OPPOSITE

Top: At the Kumbh Mela *2001. This greatest of all festivals reached its present form in the British period, but its forerunner was perhaps the 'great synod' described by the ancient Greeks, and by the Chinese in the same place in the 7th century AD. Below: Sadhus queue up to bathe at the* sangam, *the junction of the sacred rivers, at the most auspicious moment astrologically for 144 years.*

tirthankars (great saints), but the muni (guru) of Chandragupta Maurya himself, Sthula-badra who is said to have died here. In this almost forgotten corner of his imperial city, perhaps a real connection and a living tradition has survived from the age of Alexander the Great.

The Jain tradition brings us to the most fascinating of many legends about Chandragupta. After a life of great deeds and conquests, so the story goes, he resigned his kingship to become a Jain monk. The custodian of the Kamaldah shrine tells me what happened as we sit on a golden evening overlooking the lake at Patna against a distant background roar of rush-hour traffic and the claxons of crowded commuter trains. The tale that the Jains still tell goes like this. At the height of Chandragupta's rule, a Jain teacher warned him of the limits of his power. Soon afterwards a terrible famine decimated the population, and, despite all his caparisoned elephants, his vast palaces, his numberless bodyguard and his magnificent tiger hunts, the king was powerless to prevent it. He sat in his gilded throne-room while the smell of death and the sound of lamentation rose up from the streets. Eventually he summoned the teacher and submitted to him as his guru. Chandragupta's son Bhimbisara would become king, and he himself would take the cloth and begging bowl. With that, he said goodbye to his palace staff and his family, and walked out of the gates on a pilgrimage that led him far south into the rugged mountains of the Deccan. There he ended his life by ritually fasting to death in a cave at the most sacred Jain site of Sravanabelgola. This is still a great place of pilgrimage today. In 2006 millions of Jains from all over the world gathered for the twelve-yearly *mela*, pouring great vats of coconut milk, sandal paste, saffron and vermilion over the giant statue of Bahuballi (an ancient Jain guru who also renounced his kingdom). He is depicted standing naked and impassive, rapt in contemplation as the creepers grow around his body, his eyes fixed on what lies beyond. In one dramatic image, the statue encapsulates the ancient Indian faith in the power of knowledge to break the bonds of human existence.

All around this magical landscape are rocky hills and weathered outcrops where Jain ascetics still live, making offerings to images of the gurus and living on rice and pulses. On one crag the cave where the great Chandragupta passed his final days is still pointed out , its entrance smoothed by the fingers of centuries of pilgrims. On the floor is a worn carving of stone feet and a scatter of pale rice grains and hibiscus petals stirred by the warm breeze. Fierce light floods in from the cave mouth. Here the former king died, his body wasted to skin and bone, his mind floating above the emerald green hills.

'Chandragupta Maurya came here to find *moksha* [salvation],' one pilgrim told me. 'He did penance here, and when one does penance one does not eat. And so he died. But he found *moksha*.'

PREVIOUS PAGES

The Sravanabelgola mela *in 2006 when millions of Jains from all over the world gathered to pour great vats of milk, paste, saffron and vermilion over the giant statue of Bahuballi.*

Ashoka and the rule of reason

The first great political genius of Indian history, Chandragupta, died in about 297 BC. His son Bhimbisara extended the empire further, justifying his name, the 'killer of foes'. There are even later Tamil legends of a Mauryan attack on the southern kingdoms of the Cholas and Pandyas. Bhimbisara also continued diplomatic relations with the Greeks. One delightful tale tells of his request to Antiochus of Syria to purchase consignments of figs, Greek wine and a Greek teacher of rhetoric. Antiochus sent him the fruit and wine with a note saying that 'unfortunately Greek law does not permit the sale of professors'!

Then, in 268 BC, following a power struggle after Bhimbisara's death, Chandragupta's grandson Ashoka came to power. Ashoka is one of the great figures in history, and his story is told across southern Asia and the Far East in legends, folk plays and wisdom literature in the manner of the Western tales of King Arthur or Charlemagne. As a young man, the legends say, he was unattractive and ungainly in appearance, with bad skin, and was disliked by his father. But he was a capable administrator and was made viceroy of Ujain. While living there, he met and fell in love with the beautiful daughter of a merchant from the town of Vidisa, a woman called Devi. They had two children, though there is no suggestion that they married. Both the children, a boy called Mahinda and a girl called Samghamitta, are later associated with Ashoka's Buddhist mission to Ceylon. Indeed, it is Buddhist sources from Ceylon that say Devi herself was a Buddhist. They also claim that she was a member of the Sakya clan, a branch of the Buddha's family, who had emigrated to Vidisa. Whether this connection with the Buddha is a fiction or not cannot now be decided, but Buddhist tradition insists she was Ashoka's inspiration in eventually adopting Buddhism.

When Ashoka eventually became king (he was perhaps now in his thirties), Devi stayed in Vidisa rather than moving

BELOW

Ashoka, subject of novels, histories, cartoons, and even a recent Bollywood movie since his career was rediscovered in the 20th century.

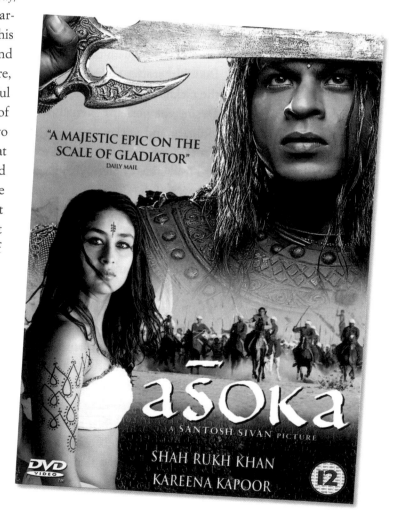

RIGHT AND ABOVE

*Sanchi, the greatest
surviving stupa of
thousands originally
built by Ashoka, rebuilt
in the 1st century BC.
What connection
the place had with
the Buddha's life is
unknown, though
Ashoka was viceroy in
the nearby town of
Vidisa, from whence
his first wife came.*

3
The Growth of Civilization

NIGHT IS FALLING off the shore of Cranganore, close enough to the Kerala coast to waft the fresh smell of palm forests after rain. Our boat is a 120-foot ocean-going *uru*, the same size as the Roman ships that plied between the Red Sea and India 2000 years go. Ours is a boat out of Cuddalore, with a Tamil-speaking crew, trading between the Andamans, Sikkal in Gujarat and the Gulf, carrying a cargo of cement, pepper and spices. After four months at sea the crew are looking forward to the thrills of the old port of

Dubai: the steersman stirs cardamom and ginger into our coffee, spits out his *pan* and grins: 'There a man may be free!'

Trade is one of the key factors in civilization. By allowing civilizations to make contact, to share and test ideas, trade also allows them to grow. Our image of India, influenced by colonial writing and historiography, has so often been of a civilization stopped in time, stuck in the past, but in fact Indian civilization has always grown and changed through dialogue with other civilizations. The tidal waves of Indian history have produced great native dynasties, but also great foreign rulers, and receptivity to outside ideas has always been part of the Indian experience. Many of the greatest developments in the story of India have been shaped by dialogue with other civilizations, which began back in the Harappan age, when Indian ships traded with the Gulf. Contacts with the Persian world had grown intensive from 500 BC, but it was only in the last centuries BC that regular sea routes opened up between the Mediterranean and peninsular India. The opening of the Spice Route to the Mediterranean spurred contacts between Rome and the kingdoms of

PAGE 98

'There are many famous markets in India', wrote a Greek sailor in the 1st century AD 'and the time for sailing there is July.'

RIGHT

An uru *boat at sea off Kerala with a cargo of timber, pepper and spices.*

southern India, while the development of the Silk Route established contacts between China, Europe and India. This was the time of Hadrian and the Antonine emperors in the West, a time the historian Edward Gibbon thought the happiest in the history of the world. And in the beginning the chief motivation, believe it or not, was the produce of a weed: pepper.

Our boat is heading up to Gujarat via the old port of Mumbai. Indians have sailed this coast up to the Gulf since at least the third millennium BC. And in the harbours of the Indian Ocean, the picturesque old dhow ports from Oman to Gujarat and the Kerala coast, you can still touch on the commerce that became one of the earliest long-distance international trades in world history, uniting the Indian Ocean and the Arabian Sea, and opening up the sea lanes to Southeast Asia and China.

They still use the old technology too. The construction yards at Beypore near Calicut almost died in the 1980s, when their manpower and skills passed to the Gulf, where the money lay. But the old shipbuilding arts have been rekindled in recent years – for good economic reasons. The old boats quite simply are still good value. The builder's boast is that an owner will make his or her money back in four years, when the lifespan of a good boat is over forty. Construction here in Kerala was often in the hands of the Mopylas, descendants of Muslim traders and crafts-men, long naturalized, who married Indian women and had their own guilds in the Middle Ages. The *mestiry* (master builder) here, though, is a Hindu: named

Gokuldas, he is only in his thirties, and his father and ancestors were also boat carpenters 'since 500 years'.

On the forested estuary of the Beypore river his construction yard is at the end of town, behind warehouses and chandlers' shops. Inside the gates piles of cut timber and two tree trunks lie outside two enormous wooden sheds, where two boat frames, each the size of a large house, rise under a rattan roof. Beyond the fence in the somnolent heat brightly painted ferries with tall prows criss-cross the river, emerging from creeks in the palm forests fringing the other side, just as they must have done in Roman times.

'We use no plans, even for boats this size,' says Gokuldas. 'There is a lot of secret calculation and mathematics involved in the process of building an *uru*. All the secrets are passed on from father to son. That's how we do it with no technical drawing – how we make such big ships to full perfection. The curve of the ship and the overall shape and structure come from working out in the mind.'

Incredibly, here on this sleepy backwater, Gokuldas has just built one *uru* boat over 170 feet long, with a 40-foot beam. High as a three-storey house and weighing in at over 1000 tons, it has a cargo capacity of 1500 tons, and now trades between the Gulf and Gujarat. Careened and recaulked in the old dhow yards of Dubai or Sikkal, it will have a good lifespan and pay for itself many times over. 'Working the old way, we get no complaints,' Gokuldas went on. 'The boats are stable and strong, and no change is needed.'

ABOVE
The old construction techniques in the boatyard at Beypore.

This gives you a sense of the scale of ancient ocean-going shipping: the big Greek and Roman cargo boats that in the Roman period plied from Myos Hormos on the Red Sea, 120 of them every year; or the five-masted trading junks that roamed the South China Sea down to Vietnam and Java well after 1949. (You could still see them in the early 1980s, as hulks and houseboats on the Shanghai river.) Similarly, the big Arab dhows that dominated the China trade in the Middle Ages are still constructed in the yards of Karachi and Dubai, though now with engines as well as sails. Scratch below the surface of the modern world, and the old ways are still there, especially in India. This is the antithesis of globalization: the persistence of local knowledge.

At the jetty down by the river in the little port of Beypore are five big *uru* boats, the largest a vessel from Tuticorin, from whose cavernous hold a crane is unloading sacks of soda ash amid clouds of choking white dust. The ship has one big, stubby mast with a giant main spar and lateen sail; she's sailing on to the Andamans. His face burnt black by the sun, the captain offers me tea heavily spiced to hide the taste of the bad water.

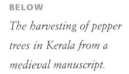

BELOW

The harvesting of pepper trees in Kerala from a medieval manuscript.

'We've sailed to the Yemen, Aden, Iraq, Iran and Somalia,' he tells me. 'From there you can come "straight over" in the summer months with the southwest wind.'

That's just as the Roman navigators used to do. Like them too, his cargo includes sacks of pepper. This is what first enticed the Greeks and Romans here.

ABOVE

Spice market on the Ganges, 1840 – a scene that can have hardly changed since Roman times.

(The word 'pepper', incidentally, like 'rice', comes from the Tamil.) At its peak, tons of the stuff were heaped in the pepper barns by the Tiber. The cost was huge. According to Pliny the Younger, 'By the lowest reckoning, the India trade takes from our empire 100 million sesterces a year – *at the lowest reckoning.* That's what our luxuries and our women cost us.' That's about 10 tons in gold – probably equivalent to the annual yield of the Roman imperial gold mines in Spain. And Pliny was perhaps only talking about the sea trade via the Red Sea, not the overland route. Interestingly enough, India is still the biggest importer of gold in the world – £9 billion worth per annum; the addiction went both ways, and still does.

The Roman craze for pepper was all about food, of course. Nothing better underlines the idea that the story of civilization is also the history of food and cooking; and Indian cooking – now a mainstay in Britain – was perhaps the first international cuisine in the world. In the Roman Empire the celebrity chef Apicius wrote a famous cookbook in which 350 of the 500 recipes – from spiced flamingo and curried ostrich to dormice stuffed with peppercorns – used pepper and southern Indian spices. Read Apicius and you get the impression that to go to a high-class dinner party in imperial Rome was to risk having your taste buds irreparably blasted. Pliny raged at the stupidity of it all: 'It's incredible that pepper has become such an obsession. With some foods the appearance is what is appealing; with some, taste or sweetness. But pepper has nothing to recommend it other than its pungency. For that we go all the way to India! Who first thought that up?'

An ancient guide to the Indian Ocean

In the pages of their geographies and gazetteers we can follow the Roman obsession down the Red Sea and all the way across to the west coast of India. The *Periplus of the Erythraean Sea*, a Greek merchant's guide to the India trade from the 70s or 80s of the first century AD, is one of them. In fact, to my mind it is one of the most fascinating of all historical texts. An old Alexandrian salt who had travelled all over the Red Sea and the Indian Ocean, Hippalos, adds his own details of winds and tides, of good and bad harbours, of where to buy and what to sell. Over the years I've tracked many of them, camping at night stops on the desert route from the Nile valley; picking over dumps of Roman pottery in sweltering Red Sea ports, such as Berenike or Adoulis; waiting in coffee shops in old Massawa, Eritrea, for the winds to change; sleeping on white sands strewn with pale crimson coral at the heavenly anchorage of Qana in the Yemen. The *Periplus* lists them all. From its pages drift the exotic substances of the ancient world: malabathron and spikenard, pepper, cloves, coral, antimony, red and yellow orpiment, along with other riches that the Mediterranean world coveted: elephant ivory, fine cotton, Chinese silk and Argaritid muslins, pearls from the Gulf of Mannar.

The *Periplus* names twenty ports on the west coast of India, but the most important in the south – Pliny calls it *primum emporium Indiae* (the first market of India) – was Muziris. This was the place where Greek navigators, beginning with Hippalos himself, made their landfall after the long direct voyage from the Red Sea. A recently discovered papyrus contract between a second-century ship-owner and an Alexandrian merchant tells us about the organization of the Muziris trade, showing how they mixed their cargoes, with several merchants bearing the costs and insurance for one voyage, 'the loan repayments as per the deal agreed at Muziris'. From the Indian side the town is recorded in Tamil poetry as Muchiri-pattanam – a *pattanam* being a 'trading port' in southern speech. A softly perfumed and much sought-after place it was too, one imagines, fanned by what the Greek sailors called the tropical *zephyrus*. A haven for lotus-eaters, maybe: a place so home from home that the Greek and Roman colonists even erected a temple to their own gods, with a special niche for the deified emperor Augustus. (So British Calcutta was by no means the first Indian city to erect statues of an emperor from the West!)

The town is marked on a beautiful, coloured Roman map called the Peutinger Table, but the location of Muziris has never been identified. We know it must have been close to Cranganore, north of Cochin, and that it lay 20 stades (2 miles) inland

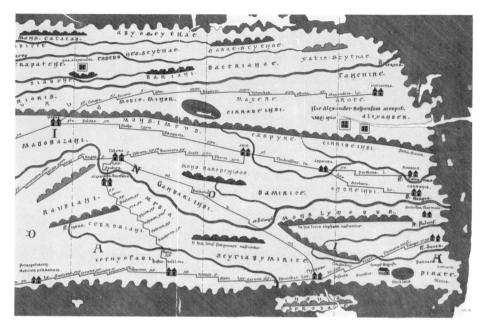

LEFT

The Peutinger Table, a map of the Roman world, showing (bottom right) the port of Muziris on the Kerala backwaters with its 'temple of Augustus'.

from the mouth of a big river, most likely the Periyar. The trouble is that rivers here alter their courses, and the Kerala coastline is notoriously prone to change, creating new shores out of sandbars and floating islands, which over time become long strands of dry land covered with forest, separating the sea from the intricate filigree of lagoons in the Kerala backwaters. But in 2005 archaeologists from Kerala found Muziris exactly where it should be. The site is now 4 miles inland, behind a double line of tranquil backwaters, and it lies by an old bed of the Periyar river, which has shifted a couple of miles up the coast since Roman times. The main mound is 650 yards across, in a shady grove of palms, bananas and jackfruit, festooned with twining pepper vines. Coins of Nero and Tiberius have been found near by, and a preliminary excavation has revealed that the mound is stuffed with Roman amphorae, broken terracotta pots, Mediterranean glass ornaments and precious stones. On top stands a very ancient brick shrine of the goddess '2000 years old' according to a local man. Her name is Pattana Devi, and her village is Pattanam, no doubt the site of the famous port known to the Greeks and Romans as Muziris.

Cosmopolitan influences

The town of Muziris had a quay and warehouses, with Arab and Jewish quarters. It was a foreign enclave, perhaps resembling those Roman trading ports in the Red Sea and Indian Ocean that are specified in the ancient gazetteers and geographies as 'designated ports' – that is, places set up under treaty with the local rulers.

The native town must have sprawled among the palm groves near by, rather as the British in their day laid out their 'Black' and 'White' towns.

So Kerala has long been a cosmopolitan place. No wonder, then, that this coast is so rich in traditions. The Arab trade with Kerala began long before Islam, and the earliest mosque in India is said to be the pretty old wooden prayer hall at nearby Cranganore, where the imam tells a story that the mosque was built by Muslim merchants, companions of the Prophet, who traded here even in the Prophet's lifetime. The Jewish community has been here at least from Roman times, originally sailing down the Gulf from Charax, near Basra, bringing with them their Iraqi rituals, and even the ancient board game excavated in third millennium BC Ur, which until recently was still played by old Indian Jewish ladies in Cochin. The Jewish trade with southern India in spices, pharmaceuticals and dyes can be traced through the Middle Ages in the fascinating traders' letters that have survived from the *geniza*, the storeroom of the Jewish synagogue in Old Cairo. During the nineteenth century Baghdadi Jewish families, such as the Sassoons, built spice warehouses in 'Jewtown' in old Cochin. Even today there are still a few Indian Jews in the vicinity of Muziris, with a lovely pillared synagogue in the forests close by at Chendamangalam.

Near Eastern Christians also settled here on the Malabar coast very early on. Exactly how early is not clear. The Apostle Thomas is supposed to have landed at the Periyar river around 50 AD with the aim of introducing Christianity to India, and a gleaming white Syrian Christian basilica stands on the spot today. The earliest Greek traditions place him – more plausibly perhaps – up in the Indo-Greek court at Taxila in the Punjab. But Muziris was a major trading place for the merchants of the eastern Mediterranean in the first two or three centuries AD, and the landing of a Roman-Jewish traveller on the Periyar river around the time of the *Periplus* is certainly plausible. It is an idyllic spot where, no doubt, many Jews, Christians and Arabs from Palestine made their landfall in the heady days of the Roman spice trade, and as evensong drifts over the swaying cocoa palms by the church of Mar Thoma (St Thomas), who would wish to doubt it?

Today red-and-green-painted passenger ferries chug across the estuary from one landing point to another; the evening catch is landed; and ladies in billowing lemon or scarlet saris skip on to the landing stage and hurry home with their shopping. It is easy to imagine foreigners settling here of all places in India, servicing the annual influx of Western boat crews. Here they could enjoy their home comforts – wine from Arezzo or Kos, Italian olive oil and fish paste (imported in the amphorae found all over the site of Muziris) – happily melding their own gods with the native ones. Is that how an Indian ivory statuette of the goddess Lakshmi found its way to Pompeii, where it was buried in the eruption of AD 79? Tamil poetry of the later Roman period talks of the Greeks as mercenaries, merchants and even sculptors in southern India. It was the beginning of a long love affair.

The spice trade between India and the Mediterranean lasted until the fourth century, when it was taken over by the Persians, and then by Arabs and Arabic-speaking Jews in the seventh century after the advent of Islam. But it left many remains, both in material traces and in ways of seeing the world. Roman coins have long been found in the antique dealers trays in Cochin, Trichy and Karur. Even today it is the custom in southern Indian marriages to give the bride a necklace of small gold coins, as it was in ancient times when the coins bore the heads of Trajan and Hadrian. Another Indian borrowing is even more curious: it is an Indian source that claims a Mediterranean origin for the oil lamp – the 'Yavana [Greek] light'. If true, how delightful that one of the greatest pleasures in southern Indian temples today should come from the homely terracotta lamp found over so many Roman sites, from Hadrian's Wall in chilly northern England to balmy Muziris: the wise maiden's lamp of first-century Palestine still burns as the flame at puja time in India's tropical south.

Madurai: the first great civilization of the south

The early train from Quilon climbs away from the sea coast of Kerala and winds eastwards through the forested hills of the Western Ghats. At Tenkasi Junction we head north by road into the plain of Madurai, passing through Srivilliputtur, where the magnificent gate tower of the Vishnu temple soars 250 feet over the little town. Bursting with sculpture, its giant medieval halls are carved with scenes from the *Mahabharata*, the national epic. For travellers arriving from Kerala the temple is their first glimpse of classic Tamil architecture, as characteristic of India's south as the Gothic cathedral is of Europe.

Marco Polo spent two months here in 1273, and he found it 'the most noble and splendid province in the world'. Approaching Madurai in the early morning before the onset of the heat, you can see why. The sky is clear and the air fresh, and apart from a gentle haze over the city, you can see all the way to the giant brown rock of Tirupparakunram, the home of the god Murugan, whose hill shrine there has been celebrated in Tamil poetry and song since the Roman period. We skirt

the city and reach our lodgings, an old British house on the wooded edge of Pasupatimalai (wild beast hill). From there a magnificent view opens out over the whole of the Vaigai plain, like a natural theatre widening out into the blue haze in the direction of the Bay of Bengal 50 miles or so eastwards. From the Kerala coast we have crossed the bottom of the Indian peninsula. This plain was the heartland of Pandyan civilization, the southernmost of the three great historical cultures of Tamil Nadu, and the mightiest power in southern India at the time of the Roman spice voyages. Down below us, at the heart of this ancient and renowned city, are the towers of the great temple of Minakshi.

Madurai is one of most fascinating places in India. The second city of Tamil Nadu after Madras, it is a thriving commercial city of a million people, with textile mills and transport workshops. Auto-rickshaws buzz up the narrow lanes around the temple like angry hornets in a cacophony of horns. Today the city is as famous as it was in ancient times for its busy commerce and its craftsmen quarters with goldsmiths and tailors. New buildings are going up everywhere, but the modern city is still shaped by its ancient layout and by the ritual calendar of a traditional

civilization. The streets form a series of concentric circles around the temple, a layout that has always determined the city's topography and that probably goes back to at least Roman times. The inner streets are named after the Tamil months, and were part of the pattern of the city from its earliest days. This is city planning as laid out in the religious Shastras. The idea of a sacred city is an ancient one, but most, such as the Forbidden City of Beijing, exist only as museums. Here in Madurai it is still a vibrant, living entity.

At the heart of the city is the great temple with its huge gate towers and labyrinthine corridors. In my experience, it's a building hard to beat anywhere in the world for sheer atmosphere. It's a Shiva temple, but is actually dedicated to Shiva's wife, who is still regarded as the real patron of the city. Here she is called Minakshi, 'the fish-eyed goddess', a very archaic name, which probably goes back deep into the cultural and linguistic prehistory of the south. The goddess of the city is mentioned in Tamil poetry as far back as the Roman period, but her name and attributes may point to a more distant connection with the culture of the Bronze Age and before.

The culture here grew over many centuries, and to sketch its background we need to go back for a moment to the aftermath of the Indus cities, the age of the Rig-Veda in the north. Here in the south the first recognizable culture begins in the Pandyan lands on the coast, 50 miles south of Madurai at the mouth of the Tambrapani river. Excavations here at Adichanallur over a century ago found a large, megalithic settlement dating back before 1000 BC, with clear links to later Tamil culture. Particularly striking was evidence for the worship of a male god, whose emblems were a leaf-bladed lance and a peacock – very like the Tamils' favourite god today, Murugan, the 'red one', the lord of the hills. There were even signs of devotees piercing their jaws with mouth-locks, a custom still practised. The excavation was reopened in 2005 with immediate and fascinating results. Archaeologists uncovered a mud-brick fortification wall faced with stone, a potters' quarter, a smithy, a place for bead manufacture, and numerous high-status burials in a huge burial ground extending over some 150 acres. Among the most remarkable of the new finds were pieces of a burial urn beautifully appliquéd with raised motifs depicting a horned deer with raised tail, a crocodile, a crane sitting on a paddy stalk, a sheaf of standing paddy, and the tall, slender figure of a woman with palms spread out – perhaps the earliest examples of art in the south yet known.

The finds at Adichanallur strongly suggest that some living Tamil traditions, such as devotion to Murugan, are very archaic indeed: so too, no doubt, is the bull-running festival, which draws 2 million people every year to Madurai and is mentioned in early Tamil poetry. The sensational find in 2006 of a votive stone axe head bearing four signs in the Indus script, unearthed on the Cavery river near the ancient town of Mayavaram, has added to these tantalizing hints. Deposited in the Iron Age, but probably an older heirloom, how it got there is a moot point. Did it come after the Indus age? Was it brought by migrants or by trade? Was the stone itself quarried in the north or the south? The find might even point to the ancient links with the northwest claimed in the oral traditions of some surviving clans and castes in the deep south, one of which (close to Adichanallur) in a poem of the Roman period is credited with an ancestry going back forty-eight generations!

This Iron Age culture developed in the last centuries BC into an urban civilization with writing that was adopted after contact with the Mauryan Empire in the third century BC. The three historical kingdoms of the south – Cholas, Pandyas and Pallavas – emerge into the light of history at that time in the edicts of the emperor Ashoka. But already Megasthenes in 300 BC had information about the Pandyan kingdom, whose goddess, he was told, was 'a daughter of Heracles', and whose army could muster 500 war elephants, 4000 cavalry and (improbably) 120,000 infantry. Nevertheless, it is clear from Ashoka's edicts that these were sizeable and powerful kingdoms. Lying beyond the Krishna river and the austere

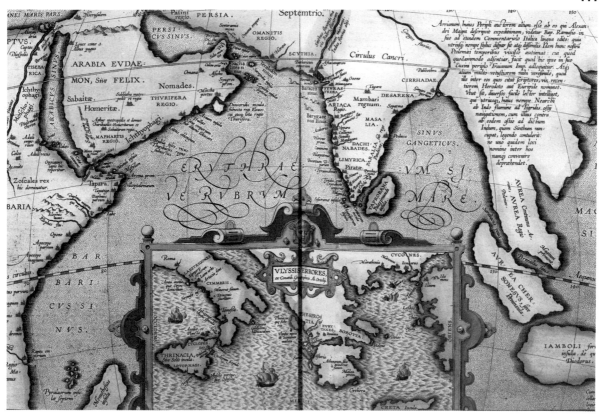

fissured plateau of the Deccan, it was never possible for the Mauryans to incorporate them into their empire. All of this helps us to understand the amazing cultural continuities of the south.

Western contacts with early Tamil kingdoms

The Pandyan kingdom was known to the Greeks from the first century BC, and Madurai later appears on Ptolemy's world map. In return, Greeks appear in Tamil poems – as royal mercenaries living in some sort of colony, and walking around the streets gawping like tourists: 'dumb *mlecchas*' (foreigners). There are even fascinating references to Graeco-Roman sculptors working here, a picture coloured by hoards of Roman coins picked up in the city and across Tamil Nadu – further proof of commercial links with the Roman world, which we saw in Muziris. In 21 BC, during the reign of Augustus, a Pandyan embassy went from Madurai all the way by sea to Rome.

The cultural pre-eminence of Madurai dates from this period. Tradition holds that the city was the centre of the *sangam*, or academy, of Tamil poets. In Tamil

ABOVE

'In earlier times', wrote the Greek historian Polybius (2nd century BC), 'the world's history consisted of a series of unrelated episodes, in widely separated localities, but from this point history becomes an organic whole: the affairs of Europe and Africa are connected with those of Asia and Greece, and all events bear a relationship and contribute to a single end.'

literature there are, in fact, legends of several still earlier, antediluvian *sangams*, but the one in the Roman period is real enough. Already in the second century BC this poetic tradition was the subject of linguistic analysis: the *Tolkapiyam*, the earliest Tamil treatise on grammar and poetics, presupposes older and now lost poetry. Only fragments of the corpus survive, among them the *Purananuru*, an anthology of 400 poems of love and war from the first century AD, which draws on the work of 150 poets. These are written-down performances of a class of poets, male and female, that was building on an oral tradition. The works include praise poems to kings on events, deeds and battles – robust, bloodthirsty and life-loving – completely different in tone from the great medieval tradition of Tamil devotional poetry that came to dominate popular culture in the south. Although already influenced by the Brahminical culture of the north, the picture they portray of the early Tamil kingdoms gives us a hint of the culture of pre-Aryan India. It is plainly no accident that the Tamil anthologies of the Roman period contain not only great poetry about war, but also about love; relationships between men and women are depicted with great psychological realism and sexual explicitness.

> What could my mother be to yours?
> What kin is my father to yours anyway?
> And how did you and I meet ever?
> But in love our hearts are as red earth and pouring rain:
>   mingled beyond parting.

Another fascinating aspect of this early Tamil literary tradition is that the city itself is a subject of poetry, a place of glamour, riches, luxuries and overseas contacts; of freedoms, social and sexual. Urban life opened up horizons, physical, cultural and mental, and there are great descriptions of crowded bazaars, temples and debating halls. The foreign presence is hinted at through mentions of Greek mercenaries and references to the consumption of foreign wines by Tamil kings and chieftains. A famous *sangam* poem, 'The Garland of Madurai', paints a brilliant image of the city in the days of the Pandyan king Nedunjeliyan. Then, it was said, the city could be smelt from miles away by the perfume of flowers, ghee and incense: 'a city gay with flags, waving over homes and shops selling food and drink; the streets are broad rivers of people, folk of every race, buying and selling in the bazaars, or singing to the music of wandering bands and musicians'.

In one passage the poem describes the stalls around the temple, selling sweet cakes, garlands of flowers, scented powder and betel *pan*. In another it lists some of the craftsmen working in their shops – 'men making bangles of conch shell, goldsmiths, cloth dealers, tailors making up clothes; coppersmiths, flower-sellers, vendors of sandalwood, painters and weavers'. All this could be today's city, as Madurai has known an amazing continuity from that time to this: the Pandyan dynasty had its ups and downs, but a distant scion of the dynasty that ruled when Greeks and Romans were here was still ruling when the British Raj took over in 1805.

Throwing light on a lost classical civilization

Tamil literature is as rich as any in western Europe – only Greek and Latin are older. However, the Tamil literature of the late Roman and early medieval periods was largely lost until the nineteenth century, and some that was written by Jains and Buddhists was lost for good. As print took over, Western forms of education came to the fore and their European Christian canons of literary value deemed the old palm-leaf manuscripts to be no longer of worth, so they were destroyed. In the mid-nineteenth century the task of recovering those lost writings began when the scholar Swaminath Aiyar, a young student at the time, met a district magistrate who revealed that manuscripts of the ancient classics still survived. As Aiyar describes in his great autobiography (1941), over the next few decades he laboriously criss-crossed the south by train and bullock cart, gathering up ancient palm-leaf manu-scripts before they were thrown out or burnt as rubbish. To his utter amazement, as he delved around temple towns such as Kumbakonum, he even stumbled upon living chains of tradition, such as the annual readings of ancient poems by the Tamil Jains, a tradition of expounding that I was astounded to discover even now (just) survives in some small Jain communities in rural Tamil Nadu.

Today, of the canonical five epics most admired by the scholars of the Middle Ages, two remain lost, and one has yet to be translated from Tamil. But although much of the early poetry has been lost, even today manuscripts are still being found in private hands, as I discovered while we were filming, when a Tamil scholar I had contacted in Madurai phoned me with a new discovery. We arranged to meet at the Minakshi temple one gorgeous spring morning, light slanting across the gate towers and glinting on the golden roof of the goddess's shrine. We sat down under a neem tree in a small, sunlit courtyard near the temple office, while Dr Sivakkolundu carefully unwrapped a manuscript that had come from an old family in a village outside the city. The manuscript was an eighteenth-century copy of the epic called *Silapaddikaram*, which was composed in the fourth or fifth century, and is set partly in Madurai.

The leaves were tied together on a loop in long, thin strips. The text had been incised with a sharp metal point, then rubbed with lamp black to bring out the letter forms. *Silapaddikaram* is rather like one of the late Shakespearean romances:

a tale of love and passion, mistaken identities, shipwrecks and sea changes, and fateful coincidences. It's a tale whose characters and locations reflect the age of the *Periplus*: wealth made on overseas voyages, grand mansions, captivating courtesans, precious gems, fine clothes … There are the young lovers, the captain's daughter Kannaki, she of 'a body like a golden creeper', and the merchant's son Kovalan, who was 'Murugan incarnate'. At the centre of the tale, malign as Desdemona's handkerchief, is the lost anklet that brings disaster on its possessors. And the background is the age when international commerce was opening up, when 'handsome great ships of the Yavanas came splashing on the foam' to the greatest port on the Tamil coast, Puhar, or Kaveripatnam. This morning, as the sun rises over the brightly painted *gopuras* (gateways), and temple bells ring deep in the interior, Dr Sivakkolundu begins to read India's oldest living classical language:

> Great and renowned kings envied the immense wealth
> > of the seafaring merchants of the opulent city of Puhar.
> Ships and caravans from foreign lands poured
> > in abundance rare objects and diverse merchandise.
> Its treasure would be untouched through the entire world,
> > bound by the roaring seas.
> The lotus-eyed Kannaki and her loving husband were fortunate:
> > they were high-born and, like their fathers, heirs to untold riches …

The tale moves between Madurai and the now-vanished city of Kaveripatnam, whose temples and 'tall mansions' stood at the mouth of the Cavery river before they were washed away by the sea or covered in dunes. Now underwater archaeologists are scouring the shallow seabed to find fragments of broken buildings. In the hinterland, down wonderful forested lanes, are ancient red-brick foundations of lost palaces, and old temples where the priests still tell legends of the fabled city that sank into the sea: the 'emporion Khaberis', as Pliny and Ptolemy call it. The Tamil epics celebrate it as 'the city of Puhar, which equalled heaven in its fame and the Serpent World in its pleasures', a town crammed with foreign merchandise 'which came by ship and caravan … Himalayan gold, pearls from the South Seas, red coral of the Bay of Bengal, the produce of Ganges and Cavery, grain from Ceylon and the rarest luxuries of Burma'.

BELOW

A palm-leaf strip with text etched by a sharp point then rubbed with lampblack. This was written for me by a Tamil scholar, Dr Sivakkolundu, to show how the ancient manuscripts were made.

ஆசிவங்கொழுந்துகளவுலர்

New worlds: the trade with China

Combine the Tamil poems with the Greek and Roman gazetteers, contracts and geographies, and together they tell us a big story about India opening up to the world. But the *Periplus* also offers fascinating clues to the very beginning of Indian commerce with China. According to the *Periplus*, it was the Tamils who ran the trade up the east coast of India, with big, sea-going catamarans made of split logs. Sailing north from the Tamil lands along the coast to Orissa, says the author,

> … the shore begins to curve eastwards, ocean on right, land on left;
> then eventually the Ganges appears in sight … the greatest river of
> India, which has a seasonal rising like the Nile. On it is an important
> trading post with the same name as the river, Ganges town, through
> which are exported malabathron and spikenard and pears, and the
> finest quality muslins called 'Gangetic'. Beyond this country there lies
> a very great inland place called China, from which raw silk and silk
> yarn and Chinese cloth are brought overland …

The port of the Ganges mentioned by the Greek navigator, where goods were transported by land towards China, we now know from recent excavations was Tamluk, which stood, and still stands, on a tributary of the Hooghly river 30 miles south of Calcutta in West Bengal. Now silted and overgrown with palm forests, this is one of those fascinating forgotten corners of India. It was once ancient Tamralipti, where a thriving port existed from Ashoka's day. Mentioned by the geographer Ptolemy in the second century AD, it became a famous Buddhist city and a major centre of scholarship, with twenty-two monasteries when the famous India traveller Hsuan Tsang stayed here in the seventh century AD. Indian and Chinese accounts show that this was the most important jumping-off point for China because it stood at the junction of three great trade routes. First was the sea route we have just travelled, down the east coast to southern India and Sri Lanka and across the Arabian Sea to the west. Then there were the two ancient routes to China: the sea route across the Bay of Bengal to Java, Sumatra and Indochina, and the land route through northern India across the Himalayas to Khotan on the Silk Route. Still an important Buddhist town in the seventh century, the port is marked on Chinese gazetteers and portolans as late as the fifteenth century, but lost its

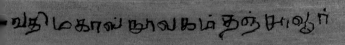

ABOVE

A Buddhist carving
of the Buddha giving
a sermon on a branch
of the Silk Road. From
the 1st century AD the
Chinese Buddhist
missionary journeys to
India would be a great
influence in the history
of China and east Asia.

importance when it silted up, to be superseded by the East India Company's Diamond Harbour, and ultimately by Calcutta itself.

We have reached a fulcrum point of history, then. 'The city of the Ganges mouth' was a junction of world trade routes on the verge of a new world order; it is the last place in the *Periplus*, which stops here after listing the ports all the way from the Red Sea to East Africa as far as Zanzibar, Arabia, the Gulf and the coasts of India. From there onwards the routes were then still unknown: 'This China is not easy to reach,' concludes the author of the *Periplus*, sitting with the old salts in his taverna on the shores of the Mediterranean around AD 70 ('like frogs around a frogpond', as Plato said). 'People seldom come from it, and not many go there.' Beyond that were only travellers' stories of migrants, nomadic traders who carried goods over the passes to China. Our sailor from Alexandria, the 'capital of memory', ends with this enigmatic final note: 'The lands beyond these places [i.e. China], on account of excessive winters, hard frosts and inaccessible country, are unexplored – perhaps also on account of some divine power of the gods ...'

So that is where geographical knowledge stood in the 70s of the first century AD. But knowledge was about to expand with astonishing rapidity as the Silk Route opened up and the first direct contacts were made between East and West. For at the very same moment that the old navigator put down his pen in Alexandria, events were unfolding far to the east that would open up another spectacular phase in the story of India – an incredible tale of lost treasures, forgotten empires and personal drama – the tale of an empire that may have been as influential as the Mughals or the British, but that is almost unknown today. And the tale begins far from India, near the border of China, beyond the Han dynasty's first Great Wall, where a people the Chinese called Yueh-chi were defeated in battle and driven westwards around the scorching wastes of the Taklamakan desert, to a new destiny and a place in world history.

The long march of the Kushans

These days we are used to understanding human geography, making our mental maps in terms of the boundaries of nation states. Most of history, though, has not been like that. Often the migrations and movements of peoples have resembled matter dissolving and re-forming, coalescing, spreading huge distances across the face of the Earth. Standing at the centre of the Old World, India has experienced such flux from prehistory to the present. Although often portrayed as a static civilization, resisting change, India has, in fact, been amazingly fluid and dynamic: the borders of her civilization have spread far beyond the boundaries marked on today's maps. Dravidians, Aryans, Greeks, Turks, Afghans, Mongols, Mughals, British … all played their part, bringing new languages, cultures, foods and ideas to the deep matrix of Indian identity. The tides of her history have been a constant interaction between the indigenous and the foreign. And so it was with the Kushans, whose tale opens almost incredible vistas, even by Indian standards.

The story begins out in the wastes of the Taklamakan desert in Xinjiang, central Asia, under the eroded fingers of the Flaming Mountains in the burning oasis of Turfan and the gravel wastes of Lop Nor. Here a strange discovery was recently made: the mummies of red-haired people of Caucasoid physiognomy, whose writings preserved in Buddhist caves reveal that they were speakers of an Indo-European language, the easternmost of the huge language group related to Sanskrit, Greek and the Western languages. Among the various names these people gave themselves, one is still (astonishingly) remembered by today's farmers near the banks of the Jumna river south of Delhi at Brindavan, the town of Krishna. Here, at Tochari Tila (the mound of the Tocharians), a family shrine was built by their rulers at the height of their power, when they ruled from central Asia to the Ganges. We know them as the Kushans, for reasons shortly to be explained.

Their first appearance in history comes in the annals of the Chinese historians, who call them Yueh-chi, a people threatening the edge of China in the wilderness beyond the mud-brick predecessor of the Great Wall, whose remains still snake out into the sandstorms of the Taklamakan from the Gate of Heaven at Jaiyuguan. This first wall of China had been built by the Han dynasty around 200 BC to keep out such peoples, nomads and migrants. The Chinese tell a terrible legend of a treacherous parley, in which they murdered the paramount chief of the Yueh-chi and made his skull into a drinking cup. Assailed by Chinese armies, the Yueh-chi packed their tents and moved westwards into the Tarim basin, the lands above Tibet. There for a while they ruled in Khotan, before their migration further westwards into central Asia and Bactria between the 160s and 120s BC.

Within a century they had established themselves as a power in the region of the Oxus river north of the Hindu Kush. The Chinese then speak of them as 900,000 people in four great tribal groupings, one of which gives us the name by which we know them today: the Kushans. Chinese chronicles mention a king whom we know as Kujula Kadphises, the first significant ruler of the dynasty. He unified the 'great Yueh-chi tribes' and invaded the Kabul valley, Gandhara and Kashmir, before dying at the age of eighty, perhaps around AD 80. Over the next ten or twenty years his son Vima Takto added northern India to the Kushan realm, and 'from this time,' say the Chinese, 'the Yueh-chi became extremely rich'. By now we pick them up in Western sources: Greek historians, who report that Bactria, the old province of the Persian and Greek empires in northern Afghanistan, had fallen to mysterious outsiders. So by the late first century AD, just the time that the *Periplus* gives us its wonderful portrait of the world between the Mediterranean and the Indian Ocean, Kushan power had extended from Bactria across the Hindu Kush into Gandhara and northwest India. In a relatively short time the Kushans had become a world power and come to control two of the most important land routes in Asia.

Once in Afghanistan and the Indus valley, when they came into contact with Indian and Indo-Greek civilizations, Kushan culture began to undergo an extraordinary transformation. The Indo-Greek kingdoms in those parts had long been multilingual, even minting coins using Greek and Sanskrit. Now the Kushans adopted the Greek script and language for their own inscriptions and coins. Then, in the early second century, they introduced their own 'Aryan' language, but still using a modified Greek script. Their language, which we know today as Bactrian, has only recently been deciphered with the help of new inscriptions, and an astonishing cache of letters, deeds and other documents written on leather, cotton and wood, from a Kushan site north of the Hindu Kush. These finds also reveal that their language continued to be used for centuries in northern Afghanistan, into the

Islamic period, and it is fascinating that there are many words from it still in common speech there today, including some deriving from Greek.

From the Hindu Kush and the Kabul valley the Kushans, within a generation or two, came down from the Khyber to Peshawar, crossed the Punjab and overran northern India as far as Mathura on the Jumna. Exactly when and how this happened is still unknown. According to the Chinese account of the rise of the Kushans, a son of Kujula Kadphises was the conqueror, who then 'appointed a general to rule India on his behalf'. This was surely Vima Takto, who minted coins with a Greek inscription that called him 'Kings of kings – great saviour'. It may have been Vima who inaugurated a new era in AD 78, which survives as the Shaka era and is found today on the front page of Indian newspapers alongside the AD dating of the Christian era. With that the Kushans could justifiably call themselves 'kings of India'.

That remarkable tale has been pieced together only recently with the decipherment of the Bactrian language; and into that picture we can now place some of the most tantalizing and brilliant archaeological finds of the modern era, the most amazing being made at Bagram, north of Kabul, on the eve of the Second World War.

The treasure of a forgotten empire

Bagram, near Charikar. The giant airstrip that formerly belonged to the Soviets in their war against the Afghan resistance is now the US military base in their war on the Taliban, where giant Hercules transport planes thunder in day and night, and F-116s rise into the sky with an ear-splitting crack. The strip lies in the plain of Kabul, and looking north there is a wonderful view towards the snow-capped mountains of the Hindu Kush. In the foreground, across green fields dotted with brown mud-brick houses – typical Afghan fortified farmsteads – a promontory sticks up over a steep drop to the Panjshir river, a place called Abdullah's Castle. The citadel is about 300 yards across, and the fortifications of the outer city are nearly half a mile further to the south. This is the site of a Greek city founded by Alexander the Great – Alexandria under the Caucasus, later known as Kapisa, the summer capital of the Kushans. Here, in 1937, French archaeologists found the greatest single hoard of artistic treasures ever discovered in Afghanistan: a wonderfully eclectic mixture of Silk Route artefacts from as far away as China and the Mediterranean, and dating from the second century. There were ivory-backed chairs of Indian origin, lacquered boxes from Han China, and Greek glass from Alexandria and Syria, including a unique glass painting of one of the Wonders of the World, the Pharos of Alexandria. There were also Hellenistic statues and silverware, stucco mouldings, and images from the Greek myths, including Cupid and the rape of Ganymede by Zeus. This extraordinary mixture is a testimony to the cosmopolitan nature of the Kushan rulers

To imagine him at Surkh Khotal in the Afghan hills is to catch a sense of a vigorous, dynamic, self-assured and egotistical man at the centre of a truly expansive age.

Discovery in the Kaffir's Castle

Kanishka's date, and even his century, have long been controversial. So too are the order and the names of those in his dynasty who ruled before and after him until their eclipse in the third century AD. But the veil has been lifted on the mystery in the last few years by an inscription found in 1993 during the Taliban war. The text, which has revolutionized the history of this period in central Asia and India, was found in the territory of Sayyed Jaffar, the local governor and head of an old Shi'ite family of Pul-i- Khumri. By a strange chance, I stayed with Jaffar after crossing the Hindu Kush to northern Afghanistan in the winter of 1995. At that time he showed me a photograph of the stone from which one could immediately see it was in the Bactrian language in Greek letters. But of its significance, no one at that stage could have been aware as the Bactrian language was still imperfectly understood. The stone had come, Jaffar said, from a place called the Kaffir's Castle, not far from Kanishka's shrine at Surkh Khotal. Deciphered in the last few years, it has turned out to be one of the most significant recent finds in early Indian history, for it is about Kanishka, not just as king of the Kushans, but as what one can only describe as the emperor of India:

> Architect of the great salvation, Kanishka the Kushan, the righteous,
> the just, the autocrat, the god, worthy of worship, who has obtained
> the kingship from Nana and from all the gods. He inaugurated the
> Year One ... and issued an edict in Greek, and then put it into Aryan
> ... In the Year One it has been proclaimed unto India, unto the whole
> realm of the ksatriyas ... his rule as far as the city of ——, the city of
> Saketa, the city of Kausambi, the city of Patna, as far as the city of Sri
> Campa ... [to] whatever rulers and other important persons who
> submitted to his will, and he had submitted all India to his will ...

The inscription has an astonishingly eclectic mix of gods: Nana and Umma, from Mesopotamia, the Zoroastrian god of wisdom Ahuramazda, and the Iranian deities Sroshard, Narasa and Mir, whose images were all placed in the royal shrine. This positively international polytheism echoes the coins of Kanishka and his son, which also depicted an eclectic choice of gods – Iranian, Greek, Indian and Buddhist. Crucially for the historian, the inscription at the Kaffir's Castle also includes a list of Kanishka's ancestors:

… for King Kujula Kadphises his great-grandfather, and for King Vima Taktu his grandfather, and for King Vima Kadphises his father, and for himself, King Kanishka, king of kings, the scion of the race of the gods … [As for] these gods who are written here, may they [keep] the king of kings, Kanishka the Kushan, forever healthy, fortunate [and] victorious, and [may] the son of the gods [Devaputra] rule all India from the Year One to the Year 1000 …

ABOVE

Discovered in the 1990s at Robotak north of the Hindu Kush, this inscription was crucial in the decipherment of Bactrian, which led to the recovery of the family tree of Kanishka and to the story of his conquest of India down to Bengal.

So now, for the first time, we have the order of the Kushan kings, and we can place Kanishka in history. He was a contemporary of Hadrian, who built the great wall across northern Britain, and of Antoninus Pius, with whom he exchanged embassies. He ruled around AD 120–150, his first year possibly AD 127. The inscription also gives dramatic new evidence about the extent of his empire: he was 'ruler of the peoples of India' all the way down the Ganges plain, from Saketa (the present-day city of Ayodhia), past Ashoka's old capital at Patna, to Sri Campa, the giant unexcavated mound of Bhagalpur in the plain of southern Bihar, which has produced a huge amount of early Buddhist material.

coins of Kanishka – relics of the days when Afghanistan was not a black hole eating up lives, armaments and munitions, but a place of peace, a bridge and transmission point of the world's cultures.

The greatest building in the inhabited world

I'm heading out of the Lahore gate at Peshawar by taxi with Zahoor on another apparently hopeless historical quest. As we've seen, Kanishka supported all religions – uncannily like other great Indian rulers, such as Ashoka, Chandragupta, Harsha and Akbar the Great, and perhaps, above all, for good, pragmatic commercial reasons in a trading empire. But he was also remembered as a pillar of Buddhism, and here in Peshawar he built what with little exaggeration one might call the eighth wonder of the world: a Buddhist stupa 300 feet across at its base and, according to Chinese pilgrims, who described its giant metal and wood umbrellas and finials, soaring 600 feet high. If these Chinese eye-witnesses are to be believed, it was the highest building yet built on Earth, and it was still standing when the monk Fa Xien came here 250 years later. 'Of all the stupas and temples the travellers saw in their journeys, there was not one comparable to this in its solemn beauty and majestic grandeur. There is a current saying that this is the finest stupa in the Jambudvipa ['rose apple continent', that is the inhabited world].'

Many miraculous stories were later told of the construction of Kanishka's stupa. One of them, repeated in legends across China and Tibet, says that the Buddha himself prophesied the stupa and the name of the king who would build it and protect Buddhism; and that when the moment came for the prophecy to come true, a magical child led Kanishka to the spot.

More details come in the AD 640s from another Chinese pilgrim to India, the famous Hsuan Tsang. But these deepen the mystery. Hsuan Tsang's extraordinarily intricate description of the structure, half a millennium after it was first built, may reflect a rebuilding after several fires, destructions and lightning damage, not the original conception. But he says the base was 150 feet high, the stupa dome itself was 400 feet high, and above it were a cupola lantern and a metal pillar with twenty-five copper umbrellas or discs. The whole structure he estimated at 500–600 feet in height. Relics of the Buddha were placed beneath the stupa by the king. A monastery was constructed on one side of the great courtyard, with a host of smaller relic stupas and shrines. By the side of the stupa in Hsuan Tsang's day there was also a great pipal tree about 100 feet high, which it was said had been grown from a sapling of the original bodhi tree at Bodhgaya.

If these stories are true, the stupa was the greatest building before the skyscraper age, soaring higher than the spire of Salisbury Cathedral or even the

LEFT

The Sufi shrine on the site of Kanishka's stupa outside the city of Peshawar. It is the latest of the Buddhist, Hindu and Muslim layers on the site.

tallest of all Gothic cathedrals, Old St Paul's in London. But could that really have been possible? It hardly seems likely, though the biggest stupa in the world today, at Nahkon Pathom in Thailand, a nineteenth-century restoration of an ancient building, stands at a staggering 412 feet. Following the clues in the Chinese pilgrims' accounts, archaeologists first went looking for its remains a century ago. The French Silk Route explorer Alfred Foucher identified the site; then a British archaeologist discovered the stupa's footings in 1908–9 and ascertained that its base was indeed nearly 300 feet across, roughly the size reported by the Chinese. But could it really have been 500–600 feet high, as the Chinese visitors claimed? It seems incredible that the technology existed to create, raise and support the vast superstructure with its copper umbrellas, though interestingly enough, the story is told that Kanishka's builders couldn't raise the great 90-foot iron post on which the umbrellas were mounted until pillars were erected at the four corners of the stupa to support scaffolding with a windlass system. Only then was the huge column lifted in the presence of the king and royal family, accompanied by prayers and libations and swirling clouds of incense. Looking at the proportion of base to height compared with other great stupas, and including flags and umbrellas, the whole structure could well have exceeded 400 feet. Certainly this would rank among the wonders of the ancient world – and even if the Chinese reports are exaggerated, construction of such a building could not have been imagined except in an age of incredible ambition and technical and artistic capability.

The site is forgotten now, a hundred years on from the British dig. It was out in the middle of open fields and graveyards then, but in the last twenty or thirty

*Gandharan Art: a
Buddhist statue typical
of the Kushan period,
mixing Greek, Indian
and Buddhist elements.*

with chunky jewellery. The Kushans, it has to be said, took the look of Buddhism – and, indeed, its ideology – into a very different place.

In the base of the great stupa at Peshawar, according to the Chinese pilgrims, Kanishka deposited a sacred relic of the Buddha himself: a casket with a small quantity of ashes. The casket, dated to the first year of Kanishka's reign, was discovered in a tiny chamber under Kanishka's stupa during the archaeological excavations of 1908–9. The tiny reliquary inside contained three bone fragments of the Buddha: these were given to the Buddhists in Burma, and remain today in Mandalay. The empty casket, though, is still here: the keeper takes it out and very carefully hands it to me. I experience a little shiver, as if the thing still has a faint charge of spiritual radioactivity. The keeper continues:

> There is some discussion today about whether it is actually of his time, or if it was put under the stupa by his successor. The text is signed by the maker, who is possibly (though there is argument over this too) an artist with a Greek name, Agesilas, who oversaw the work at Kanishka's foundation. The inscription has been read like this: 'The servant Agesilas, the superintendent of works at the vihara [shrine] of Kanishka in the monastery of Mahasena'. But other readings are possible.

The decorations on the casket form an eloquent – and intimate – testimony to the eclectic bent of the Kushans. The lid shows the Buddha on a lotus pedestal, worshipped by Brahma, the creator god of the Hindus, and Indra, the old sky god of the Rig-Veda. I turn it over in my hands. The matt bronze finish is unblemished and looks almost new. On the edge of the lid is a frieze of flying geese, Buddhist symbols of the achievement of enlightenment. On the casket itself in relief is a Kushan monarch, probably Kanishka, with the Iranian sun and moon gods at his side. The king wears the same big nomadic boots and greatcoat he wore on the smashed statue in Kabul Museum and on his vivid portrait coins – could this perhaps have been a mass-produced, 'authorized' image? On the sides are two images of a seated Buddha, worshipped by royal figures. A garland, supported by cherubs, goes around the scene in typical Hellenistic style. The casket is a tiny artefact, tucked away on one of the lower shelves in the museum, but as a symbol of the Kushan age, it's perfect.

Peshawar, it would become a main place of residence for the Kushan kings, and their winter capital. From here, according to the Afghan inscription found at the Kaffir's Castle, Kanishka mounted an expedition down the Ganges and annexed Saketa (present-day Ayodhia), Kausambi, Patna and Champa (now Bhagalpur). By then his empire dominated the heartland of Indian civilization.

Revolutions in ways of seeing

It often happens with foreign dynasties – the British and the Mughals are other cases in point – that outsiders who want to improve their understanding of the lands they rule seek to record, codify and explain the indigenous culture. Several great figures in Indian culture are associated by later tradition with Kanishka's court. In the indigenous Indian tradition of medicine, Ayurveda, the physician Caraka (or Charaka), one of its two traditional 'founders' (whose works are still passed down in lineages by oral teaching), is said to have been the guru of Kanishka, and is the subject of many legendary tales as far away as China. It is also likely that during this period revisions of the early epics the *Ramayana* and the *Mahabharata* were produced, just as they were under the Guptas, the Cholas and the Mughals, all of whom had a great interest in 'imperial ' and 'national' epics. Indeed, new evidence suggests that it may have been under the Kushans that Sanskrit, hitherto a sacred language that was the preserve of the Brahmins, began to be disseminated as a 'classical' literary language, eventually assuming the role across southern Asia that Latin would have in the medieval West.

Another important intellectual figure at this time was Asvagosh, a Buddhist teacher, who was a poet and a dramatist, but also the author of a great collection of Buddhist *jatakas* (magical birth tales), which were transmitted across eastern Asia, and have been described as the forerunners of *The Arabian Nights* and Boccaccio's *Decameron*. Asvagosh's work as a playwright is especially interesting in view of the still continuing tradition of miracle plays in Mathura. The earliest evidence for acting troupes in India comes from the Kushan age in Mathura, with inscriptional references to a courtesan from a 'family of actresses' and a travelling company of 'players from Mathura' working across northern India.

But perhaps the most fascinating product of the Kushan age is the art developed in Mathura: a uniquely cosmopolitan art that would influence the whole history of Indian and eastern and southern Asian art. Under the Kushans a revolution in Indian art took place, driven by Kushan and native Indian traditions, and by the Greek–Buddhist art of Gandhara. Its characteristics are a vigorous sense of life, a roving curiosity and an eclectic mind borrowing from many sources. It was an art that served its purpose of mass communication better than most in history to

the *Mahabharata* as an indigenous chief of Mathura. This cycle of over thirty plays developed in its present form in the sixteenth century, with all the parts played by children: and in them the central theme is of the tyrant of Mathura, Krishna's wicked uncle, who is eventually overthrown by his nephew. His name, Kans or Kansa, is still attached to many ancient Kushan mounds around the city. Could this, I wonder, be a folk memory of the great Kushan?

If so, here's a last twist. On the northern edge of Mathura, overlooking the river, is an ancient mound deep in debris, littered with fragments of Kushan Buddhist sculpture. A footpath leads up to a cluster of yellow-painted houses and a Hindu shrine of Gokarneshwar, an incarnation of Shiva. You enter through a gateway that leads into a little courtyard and a marble-floored chamber. The inner sanctum is lit by a strip light, and a fan in the ceiling gives a bit of relief in the 47-degree heat of Mathura before the monsoon. The image of the god is a giant statue of a king with great saucer-like eyes, sitting on a kind of throne, holding a wine bowl and grapes, and wearing a pointed Kushan cap. Backed with green floral tiles and holding a big brass trident, he stands in for Shiva now, with strings of wilting marigolds around his neck, his bulky shoulders covered with purple powder. But this was once a Kushan king. In the city of his demise, the 'son of the gods' Kanishka is perhaps worshipped still today.

Although virtually unknown in the West, Kanishka's legend is remembered across China, Mongolia, Tibet and Japan. Recently the king was even portrayed in one of the biggest Japanese *mangas* (adult comics), which sold 30 million copies, and has spread in cartoon versions and films to Europe and the USA. Here he is Ganishka, the grand emperor of the Kushans, head of a demonic empire, who can throw lightning bolts and who uses his familiars, his demon soldiers and his dark magic to conquer the entire world! Coming out of eastern Buddhist legends, it is a strange fate for the king who opened up the world and brought the art and ideas of East and West to Afghanistan and India; the king who sent embassies to Hadrian in Rome, and Buddhist missionaries to China.

The legacy of the Kushans

It had been an extraordinary journey. We had followed the Kushans all the way from the Merv oasis across the Hindu Kush to Kabul, Peshawar and Mathura, and the journey confirmed to me that the story of the Kushans is one of the most fascinating in history. Their empire collapsed in the third century AD under pressure from Sassanians and then Huns, but it left a permanent legacy. In northern Indian history the Kushans are the link between the ancient world and the great era of the Guptas (see Chapter 4), defining some of the key features of later Indian civilization.

OPPOSITE

Krishna is mentioned as the god of the Mathura region by the Greek Megasthenes in c. 300 BC.

4
Medieval India: Age of Gold and Iron

SUNSET FROM THE GOGRA BRIDGE in Ayodhia, a small country town in the Ganges plain: the sky looks molten – vivid red-gold underneath a huge bank of deep blue monsoon clouds. The air has freshened up with reviving rain after a muggy day, and now the evening is simply glorious. The river is rising with the coming of the rains, waves whipped up by the wind and rushing over the shallows, spreading wide to the horizon like an inland sea. To the right is open countryside, the

riverbank fringed with waving reed beds, and beyond that is what the locals call *jangal* – a wild landscape of lagoons and groves of trees through which are glimpses of a thatched village. To the left, across the bridge, are the painted domes and towers of the city: twenty or thirty mosques, tombs and temples lit up by the setting sun. On the bathing ghats pilgrims still throng, taking a last bath, squeezing out their clothes, saying sunset prayers, orange flags snapping around them in the breeze. The light dips, becoming peach-coloured; then, as the sun disappears, it fades into a soft blue. It's a beautiful sight, conjuring feelings of pure elation. One can almost believe in fairy tales, or at least see why this place was chosen by medieval poets to be the earthly location for the golden age of the Ramrajya, the rule of Rama. Golden ages, though, are problematical things, for they never exist in reality; they are imagined pasts – literary creations made for a purpose, and capable of very different readings, both creative and destructive. They perhaps tell us less about the past than about the present – and about our imagined futures.

Between about AD 400 and 1400 – in European terms, from the time of the fall of Rome to the Renaissance – Indian civilization enjoyed a series of brilliant flowerings in its regional cultures, but also went through great changes, in some places suffering violent rupture. The coming of Turkic and Afghan conquerors bearing the faith of Islam would set the north on a new path that would eventually lead India, the largest Muslim land on Earth, to be partitioned on religious grounds in the mid-twentieth century. The fact of this change is clear among the writers of those early times. At the end of the tenth century northern India ('Hindustan' to Muslim geographers) was seen as a land whose people were all 'idolaters', that is, followers of the native Indian religions – what we today would call Hindu, Buddhist and Jain – along with the many folk religions and cults. But in the Middle Ages northern India would become one of the greatest Muslim civilizations in the world, both in numbers and in creativity. (If we include Pakistan and Bangladesh, the subcontinent still has much the biggest Muslim population today.)

These changes were tremendous historical events that are still profoundly influencing the history of India. The next stage of our journey, then, takes us into those times when some of the key lineaments of modern Indian civilization were laid out: the rise of great kingdoms across India, in Bengal and Orissa, the Chandalas in Khajuraho, the Cholans in the south, all of which, though speaking different languages, saw themselves as belonging to an Indian 'great tradition', sharing the same complex of religions that since the nineteenth century has been called Hinduism. In the northwest, Muslim kingdoms were created, forerunners of the modern state of Pakistan. This was a time that saw the gradual decline and disappearance of Buddhism, except in the Himalayan regions and Bengal. Out of these great tides of history, with their waves of creation and destruction, an even more diverse India would grow. The story begins at the time of the fall of the Roman Empire, in the fifth century AD, and it led me first of all to one of India's most famous cities: a name to conjure with in Indian history, and what one recent Indian writer has called 'India's Ground Zero'.

Inside Ayodhia, the city of Rama

Early morning and the heat is already rising. The Hotel Ram lies on the edge of the sacred zone of Ayodhia. It's scruffy but friendly: in the dining room there's a tasty vegetarian breakfast of puri and vegetables with purple pickled onions – no meat, eggs or alcohol are permitted in God's city. Upstairs skinny builders in loincloths and headbands are already banging away, mixing pink cement in the bedrooms opposite mine. In the foyer a large TV sits alongside a big poster of Rama as the just king – a handsome, square-jawed young warrior, with bare chest, limpid, movie star eyes, helmet and bow. Next to him is Sita, his wife, the ideal woman, his brother Lakshman, and Hanuman, the half-human, half-monkey beloved across India, who

in the legend saves Rama in his climactic battle with the demon king. In the modern revival of Hindu nationalism that began in the 1920s and has peaked in the last twenty years, Rama has come to be seen, in northern India at least, as the supreme godhead himself, and Ayodhia is held to have been his birthplace.

Turn right out of the front door, and you are immediately in the heart of things. In a street, already heavy with sun, you walk past the corner *chai* shop, where a resident cow hovers to share customers' leftovers, and in a few yards you come to the police lines. Beyond them the sacred centre of the city stretches down to the river in a mile of fabulously crumbling lanes and alleys, a labyrinth of 300 temples, hostels, mosques and Sufi shrines. Two minutes away from what passes for calm, I find myself swept up in a scene of fantastic vitality, which goes on day and night, and it is fascinating just to wander, hang about or sip *chai* as an unending stream of pilgrims floods past, millions of them every year, all drawn by the tale of Rama.

As you walk, you notice everywhere on the stucco façades of mansions and shrines great plaster fish, their scales painted bright blue – the badge of the Muslim nawabs of Ayodhia, or Awad (as it was known). In 1722 the rulers here, who were Shi'ites, became effectively independent of the great Mughal in Delhi. Curiously enough, it was under them that most Hindu temples here were built in the century-long heyday of Awadhi culture, whose twilight is portrayed in Satyajit Ray's great film *The Chess Players* (1977). The town's greatest Hindu temple, dedicated to Hanuman, was paid for by a Muslim nawab. Since then, Ayodhia has had its ups and downs: sectarian fighting flared in 1855, first between followers of Shiva and Vishnu, then between Muslims and Hindus, but for much of the last 300 years

ABOVE

The TV Ramayana produced in the late 1980s had a tremendous effect on the popular culture and communal politics in India. In the countryside whole villages gathered to watch it on a single, battery-powered TV set.

Ayodhia was as good an exemplar of religions living together as could be hoped for in the often troubled sectarian world of northern India. But since 1992 the city's name has become associated with horrors that have threatened the whole Indian body politic. In that year, inflamed by a flagrantly sectarian campaign by their politicians, Hindu fundamentalists descended on Ayodhia in their thousands and demolished a Mughal mosque that they claimed had been built on the exact site of the birthplace of Rama himself. In the bitter aftermath, riot and murder occurred across northern India, and many of the Muslim population of Ayodhia were killed or forced to flee for their lives. That night the prime minister, Narasimha Rao, spoke to the nation on television:

> Fellow countrymen, I am speaking to you this evening under the grave threat that has been posed to the institution, principles and ideals on which the constitution of our republic has been built. ... What has happened today in Ayodhia is a matter of great shame and concern for all Indians. ... This is a betrayal of the nation, and a confrontation with all that is sacred to all Indians as the legacy we have all inherited ... I appeal to all of you to maintain calm, peace and harmony at this grave moment of crisis. We have faced many such situations in the past and have overcome them. We shall do this again ...

In the narrow lane outside Hanuman's shrine the pilgrim stalls are heaped with pictures and cassettes, and the bookshops are piled high with copies of the *Ramayana* (the famous Gita Press edition has sold an incredible 65 million copies). Long fundamental to the popular culture of northern India, the Rama legend has become a giant presence in the rise of the Hindu nationalist movement in the last hundred years, and especially since the 1980s. Originally a hero of early epic, so scholars tell us, Rama is believed by devotees to be an avatar or incarnation of Vishnu, who comes down to Earth 'at times whenever injustice thrives'. (Another famous incarnation is Krishna, but on pilgrim stalls up and down the Ganges plain one will also see images of the Buddha, and even Jesus and the Shi'ite imam Hussein portrayed among the avators).

In the north Rama's name has been used as a synonym for God since the Middle Ages. But he is also the ideal man and ideal king, an exemplar for human action. And the incredible popularity of the tale was underlined by a blockbuster TV series in the late 1980s, which in the popular eye has increasingly become the received version. In Ayodhia its seventy-eight episodes blare from every bookshop and pilgrim stand. For many, though, the astonishing success of the series was offset by a deep unease at the use to which it has been put – as the focus of a communal

rendering of Indian national history, supplanting in the popular imagination the myriad other tellings, often contradictory, unorthodox or subversive, but still part of the great *Ramayana* tradition. But in the electronic age the tale is still changing, still shaping views of the Indian past. And the town of Ayodhia is the theatre where myth has been translated into modern metaphor.

The legend of Rama

'The soil of Ayodhia has been sacred for nearly 1 million years,' the head of the temple tells me. Burly, white-bearded, his forehead marked in damp sandal paste with the yellow sign of the Vaishnavaites, like an inverted tuning fork, he has been a driving figure in the campaign to erect a temple to Rama on the site of the demolished mosque. He is sitting cross-legged in a cramped, oven-hot study heaped with pamphlets and books. Around the walls are religious images depicting the legend: gods and goddesses with jewelled crowns and kohl-rimmed eyes; Sita in a crimson sari. In the sweltering, pre-monsoon summer heat sweat beads trickle down my forehead and my shirt is soaked as the mahant continues:

An 18th-century image of the marriage of Rama and Sita: ideal husband and ideal wife, but like all the greatest stories, shot through with a dark strain of tragedy which religious interpretations have never quite been able to iron out.

We consider Ayodhia was built by the first human being, Manu, but as a human artefact, it is merely a resemblance of the eternal city of the gods. Hence its name, which means 'unconquerable'. You see, Indian time is without beginning and end, and goes beyond counting. To call one thing present and another thing past is against the idea that all is permeated by the One. What we call one moment is in fact indestructible time … We can only see the divine setting of Ayodhia with an Indian eye. The knowledge of Europe is of no avail to reach the depth of ancient India.

The mere historian feels a little powerless in the face of such certainty. But the point is that the tale told by the traditional Brahmins and pilgrim guides here takes place in another aeon. Our era, the Kali Yuga, began a mere 5000 years ago, after the great war described in the *Mahabharata*. The time of the *Ramayana*, the Treta Yuga, is much further back, nearly 1 million years ago. A different view of the tale's beginnings, though, might suggest its origins in myth and folk tale. Three figures in Indian religion and myth have the name Rama, which (like Krishna) means 'the black or dark-skinned one'. One of these is 'the bearer of the plough'. Now Sita means 'the furrow' and is the name of a goddess of agriculture in some ancient Sutras; in one text, the *Harivamsa*, she is the goddess of farmers. Perhaps these clues point to an aboriginal or pre-Aryan origin to the tale? Whatever, the tale as we have it almost certainly arose in the last centuries BC, out of oral stories and bardic tales. Its setting is quite narrow: a small area of the kingdom of Kosala, between the Ganges and the Jumna; and, for what it is worth, the sites associated with the tale have all yielded pottery of post 600 BC, later than the *Mahabharata* sites (see page 50).

There are hundreds of tellings of the story in twenty main languages across southern Asia, some offering fascinating and radical variants, but the core story, the most widely accepted, goes like this …

Rama is a prince of Kosala, residing in the city of Ayodhia in the Ganges plain. Unjustly exiled from his father's kingdom, he lives in the forest with his faithful wife Sita and his brother Lakshman. This golden time is broken when Sita is abducted by Ravana, demon king of Lanka ('island' in Sanskrit). Ravana, the charismatic, tragic anti-hero is supremely intelligent; he can appear in any guise (the most famous has ten heads and twenty arms) and cannot be killed by gods, demons or spirits. Ravana begins to lay waste the Earth and destroy the deeds of the good Brahmins, the upholders of dharma (the universal moral law), so Rama is born a human to defeat him.

Lanka is now identified with Sri Lanka, but this is not recorded as an early name of that island, and it is possible that the city of the demon king was originally

The siege of Lanka by Rama and the monkey armies shown in a 17th-century Mughal painting. The Ramayana *was a great source of interest to the Mughal emperors who commissioned translations into Persian.*

Sita tested by fire: the story of Rama has sometimes radically different endings in its many regional traditions.

envisioned by poets as much nearer to hand. More likely, though, it is a fairy-tale city, part of a geography that is not to be found on this Earth. The eleventh-century Muslim historian al-Biruni says that 'according to the Indians, Lanka is thirty yojanas above the Earth, and no sailor who has ever sailed in the direction ascribed to it has ever seen anything that tallies with the legend'. As with Homer's *Odyssey* or the *Argonautica*, over many centuries mythic geography shifts to accommodate the expansion of real geography, just as the *Ramayana's* setting in time eventually had to be put back to a mythic age a million years ago. According to the Brahmins, the *Mahabharata* was 'what happened' in the heroic age, just before 'real' history; the *Ramayana* is 'what is always', which means it is disengaged from historical chronologies. It is in another aeon, a paradigm. This is not 'history' like the *Iliad* or the *Mahabharata*, and in such myths it is best, if at all possible, that mental maps stay magical.

While living in idyllic exile in the forest, Rama offends the demonic world by rejecting and insulting the sister of the demon king. Captivated by Sita's beauty, Ravana diverts Rama with a golden deer and, disguising himself as an old holy man, abducts her. To cut a long story short, the tale ends in a great expedition to Lanka, where in a tremendous battle Ravana is overthrown with the crucial help of the faithful monkey Hanuman. Sita is restored to Rama, and in some versions rules happily ever after in Ayodhia, though only after she is tested to see if her virtue was sullied by Ravana. But the dark strain of tragedy and jealousy in the epic emerges in an ambiguous and troubling epilogue, which may in part be a later addition (and which was initially not filmed in the Indian TV version). This final denouement has all the power of the greatest myths, where the tale finally imposes its own logic of destiny on the protagonists. Just as there was a long tradition in the Greek myth that Helen never went to Troy – her actions too problematic to leave unquestioned – so it is with Sita, the heavenly wife, 'the jewel of womanhood, daughter of Earth' (as Kamban, the great Tamil poet, calls her). Further whispers about her virtue lead to her banishment by Rama, and Sita brings up their children on her own in the ashram of the sage Valmiki (who will later write down the story). Then, in the final meeting with her doubting husband, the ground opens up and swallows Sita, who is taken back by Mother Earth, just as Medea is taken back by the gods in the Greek myth. In both great mythic traditions the storytellers just couldn't leave things with a happy ending; a warning, perhaps, that golden ages exist only in fairy tales.

The Guptas and the Rama legend

But where and when was the legendary Ayodhia? And how and why did the story become, along with the *Mahabharata*, a national epic? Here in today's Ayodhia the tale about the discovery of the site of the million-year-old lost city is part of the repertoire of the pundits, the pilgrim guides, who can be hired anywhere along the bathing ghats by the Gogra bridge, as noted for example by the Elizabethan visitor Ralph Fitch, among 'certain Brahmins who record the names of all such Indians as wash themselves in the river running thereby'.

Our guide is a small, bird-like man sitting by the riverbank under a great old tree, a big yellow Vaishnavite mark on his forehead. In front of him is a cloth bag with his list of clients, and an old lithographed book of sacred texts. The tale of the founding myth of the city is first told in a text of the fourteenth century, and much the same tale is still the oral tradition, as our guide reveals:

> Once upon a time, long, long ago, there was a great king called Vikramaditya. One day Vikramaditya came hunting along the Sarayu river. Then his horse suddenly pulled to a halt, hearing strange voices, and would go no further. The king picked his way through the jungle on the hill there and found ruins of an ancient city. He cleared the ruins and then a rishi (a holy man or renouncer) appeared before him, who told him this was none other than Ayodhia, the sacred city of Lord Rama, which had existed in the Treta Yuga. Then the rishi

have ruled from the Bay of Bengal to the Indus. From their time there is a superlative but disparate series of creations: play texts and poems revealing the sophistication of courtly society; remarkable scientific findings; sculpture of wonderful quality (the sandstone Buddha of Sarnath surely has few rivals in the arts of the world). In the National Museum in Delhi there are terracottas so expressive that they might be from *fin de siècle* Paris – maquettes from the studio of Auguste Rodin, say – and in the coin gallery there is an astonishingly vivacious and technically brilliant series of gold coins. And what of the ethereal, crumbling beauty of the paintings in the Buddhist caves at Ajanta, some of which may be from this period? Or the 6-ton, forge-welded iron pillar plundered from its wooded hill at Vidisha and now in the grounds of the Qutab Minar complex in Delhi? Not to mention the world's first sex manual (something the Western world did not achieve until the 1960s). But where is the material dimension of Gupta power? Nowhere except in a few small temples can one stand and say 'Here is the Guptas' legacy'. No palaces, no public buildings, no grand shrines, only caves and ruined stupas. Virtually nothing is known about their day-to-day life, about the administration of their empire, about the execution of justice, about national and international commerce. Their kings' personalities are a mystery, but for a few high-flown eulogies. Their apparent greatness, then, presents us with a conundrum.

A golden age?

The idea of the Gupta golden age arose, curiously enough, not among Indians, but among the British. Vincent Smith was a civil servant and a brilliant historian, but fundamentally unsympathetic to many aspects of Indian civilization. His was a colonial viewpoint that helped shape British views of India. For Smith the Indians were never so happy as when held in good order under firm but benevolent authoritarian empires, such as that of the Mauryans, the Guptas, the Mughals – and the British. (And, after all, weren't the British – albeit distantly – Aryans too?) The Guptas, then, were the kind of imperialists the British empire-builders could admire as models.

The empire began with Chandragupta I (reigned 320–35), a member of a local landed family, who fought his way to power in the region. He married a princess of the Licchavi, an important clan in the northern Bihar-Patna region, with lands stretching up to Nepal. The alliance was so important to him that his son Samudragupta called himself 'son of the daughter of the Licchavi'. So where the Kushans celebrated the father's line, for the Guptas it was the uterine descent that made them. Like the Kushans, their accession was the start of a new era, beginning with Chandragupta's coronation in 320. With that, the time was renewed.

Chandragupta showed himself to be the restorer of ancient Vedic kingship by renewing the great Vedic horse sacrifice (see page 40), the roots of which are traced back to central Asia, and this act was commemorated on his gold coins. Decades later his grandson praised him as the great renewer of the horse sacrifice 'which had been forgotten for a long time'. So the Guptas were consciously trying to renew the old Vedic institutions of kingship, as a native dynasty that traced its descent, male and female, to the old clans of the Ganges plain.

The next king, Samudragupta (died 380), was (if we can believe his press) one of the greatest conquerors in Indian history. To Ashoka's Allahabad pillar he added a fulsome account of his deeds, including a long list of kings and realms conquered: fourteen border kings, eighteen jungle rajas and even thirteen southern kings. After that he proclaimed himself a *chakravartin* (universal ruler), and a new tone appears in Indian kingship: 'He was a mortal only in celebrating the rites of the observances of mankind, but otherwise a god dwelling on Earth.'

His son, Chandragupta II (reigned 380–413), extended the empire to its furthest extent, its greatest glory and cultural excellence. By then the empire stretched from the Khyber to Bengal. A poetic eulogy to him is carved on the Delhi Iron Pillar: touched with a smouldering evanescence, 'his face as beautiful as the moon … he has gone now to heaven but left behind his glory in the world, in the way that the earth still glows hot after a raging forest fire. He smashed the King of Bengal and crossed the seven mouths of the Indus to rout his enemies, so the southern ocean is still perfumed by the breeze of his bravery … '

The great kings of the line end with Skandagupta in *c.*467, though scions of the dynasty still ruled until the middle of the sixth century.

As regards real historical narrative, that would have been the lot were it not for a vivid picture of the Gupta realm written by a foreign visitor. Around 401, the same year that the iron pillar inscription was carved, a Chinese monk called Fa Xien travelled down the Karakorum into the Punjab to visit the sacred places of Buddhism. He was an eye-witness to the Gupta world at the end of the reign of Chandragupta II. At that time Buddhism was still thriving, he tells us: 'Everywhere

ABOVE

Vishnu on his seven-headed serpent: an exquisite piece of Gupta sculpture depicting the god favoured by the Gupta kings.

in all the countries of India the kings had been firm believers in that law.' Intriguingly, he tells how the Gupta kings (who were not Buddhists, but followers of Vishnu) by long tradition visited Buddhist monasteries 'to make offerings to the monks with uncovered heads, and gave food with their own hands, sitting with them on the floor: for the laws and ways according to which kings rendered charity in the days when the Buddha was alive have been handed down to the present day'.

South of Mathura the Chinese visitor travelled between the Ganges and Jumna, in the 'beautiful and fruitful' landscape that impressed foreigners, from Megasthenes to Ralph Fitch, for 2000 years. Then comes this passage:

> All south from here is known as the Middle Land or Kingdom. In it the cold and heat are finely tempered, and there is neither hoar frost nor snow. The people are numerous and happy; they have not to register their households, nor to be ruled by magistrates; only those who cultivated the royal land have to pay a tax on the gain from it. If they want to go [leave their land], they can go; if they want to stay on, they stay. The king governs without decapitation or corporal punishments. Criminals are simply fined lightly or heavily according to the circumstances of the case ... The king's bodyguards and staff all have salaries. Throughout the country the people do not kill any living creature, nor drink intoxicating liquor, nor eat onions, nor garlic ... the only exception is the chandalas. That is the name for those who are held to be polluted, and who live apart from the rest of the population ...

One must take such a eulogy with a pinch of salt; some of the details seem improbable – the non-drinking of alcohol for one – and it is curious that Fa Xien does not mention the ruling king. But much of his information is true: that untouchables had to strike a wooden stick before entering towns, as he describes later, is known from other sources; likewise the use of cowrie shells along with coins as currency, and the prohibitions on certain kinds of food. His account of the administration strikingly recalls what we know of the Mauryans.

Fa Xien later reinforces these observations on his journey further south to Patna: 'The cities and towns of this country [Maghada],' he says, 'are the greatest of all in India. The inhabitants are rich and prosperous, and vie with one another in the practice of benevolence and righteousness.' Particularly eye-catching is his description of how the citizens of Gupta Patna (whether Buddhist, Jain or Brahmin) shared each other's festivals and revered each other's teachers. As discussed in Chapter 2, despite the many conflicts over religion in Indian history, this kind of pluralism has long existed, and still continues in Patna and in many other

places. Fa Xien, then, opens a window on a well-organized kingdom that could not have been guessed at from the scanty and fragmentary material survivals, and behind it an Indian ruler who claimed to be a 'universal king'.

ABOVE

The gorgeous quality of this mural from the caves at Ajanta vividly suggests the sophisticated culture of the Gupta age.

Art, poetry and science in the Gupta age

Like other great epochs of Indian history, the Gupta age was a pluralist time. Although the kings were followers of Vishnu, they sponsored other religions, and Buddhism in particular, as the Chinese pilgrims' accounts show, enjoyed a great flowering with royal patronage. The monastery at Nalanda, with its university, was a Gupta-period foundation, the first residential university in the world. It became a global institution, drawing students from the Far East and Persia, and lasted until the twelfth century.

This was also a time of major scientific advances. Aryabhata, the astronomer and mathematician, defined the concept of zero and proved that the Earth revolves around the sun and that it turns on its own axis some 1000 years before Copernicus and Galileo expounded this idea in the West. A hallmark of the age, then, seems to have been curiosity about the world in all its manifestations. Artistic creation, especially of the human form, is another. Some of the wall paintings of the life of the Buddha at Ajanta are from this time, and some of the finest stone images in Indian art come from the Gupta period: chief among them are the sculptures made by Dinna, the first Indian artist for whom we have a name and a collection of works.

The Gupta court also sponsored literature and poetry. Later legend speaks of the 'nine jewels' in the royal court, one of whom, Kalidasa, seems to have been court poet to Kumaragupta, rather as Virgil was to Augustus Caesar. He was the author of poems, epics and plays, the most famous of which is *Sakuntala*, a charming comedy (tragedy seems to be unknown as a genre in Indian drama – perhaps the law of karma would preclude it?). The play has distant similarities to *A Midsummer Night's Dream*: the king's love for a forest nymph, the lovers' pursuit in the woods, the contrast between court and country, the fairy-tale ambience. But what is most revealing in the play is what it tells us about the courtly culture thriving in Gupta cities such as Ujain and Patna and its self-reflexive quality. The play starts in an almost Pirandellian fashion, with a prologue where the director and his leading lady discuss tonight's show:

'They are a very high-powered audience tonight, they are the intelligentsia … really discriminating … So we need to serve them up something really good …

'With your direction nothing can go wrong,' says the star, perhaps with a hint of irony.

'Unfortunately, my dear,' the director replies, 'however talented we may be, we still all crave the applause of the discerning …'

Kalidasa's three surviving plays and his lyric poems (such as the 'Birth of the War God' and his *Raghuvamsa*) flatter the Gupta line, as Shakespeare's history plays do the Tudor monarchs, and make specific homage to the current ruler. This was fitting in a time of historical consciousness, when court scholars collected and edited the texts of the Puranas, compendia of the myths, history and genealogies of the northern dynasties. The fourth book of the *Raghuvamsa* glorifies the mythical dynasty of King Rama in a eulogy to the heroic deeds of his current representative on Earth. In this way the real world battles recorded on the Allahabad pillar are turned into literary art.

So the transformation of history into myth was part of the programme of the Gupta rulers. Whereas earlier rulers in the ancient Indian tradition saw their job as being to keep the cosmic order going, performing Vedic sacrifices advised by their Brahmin priests, or, like Ashoka, propounding a moral order articulated by Buddhist or Jain gurus, now kingship itself was central to the discourse: the Gupta kings were thought to be gods on Earth, bringing about a new golden age by means of their heroic deeds in battle, but also sponsors of a court culture where arts could flourish. In style and substance it would be the template of all later rulership in India.

The Kama Sutra: sex and life

The most remarkable of all the products of Gupta culture – and, for obvious reasons, the most interesting to our sex-obsessed time – is *The Kama Sutra*, the treatise or exposition on delight, love, pleasure or sex, though as Kama is also the personified god of love, the title could simply be translated as 'The Book of Cupid'. The oldest surviving Hindu textbook on erotic love, it was composed in Sanskrit perhaps between 300 and 400. The author, Vatsayana Mallanaga, was probably writing in Patna, the old Ashokan capital, still an imperial city under the Kushans and Guptas. The cultural context of the text is urban and cosmopolitan; the target readership is the *nagaraka*, the man about town, and it gives us a fascinating glimpse (echoed in the sensuous and pleasure-loving sculpture of the age) of what India was like in the age of the Guptas.

The author of *The Kama Sutra* says his work follows many other writers in the past – earlier sexologists – but his is the first to survive. It became a landmark, being quoted as early as 400, and influenced many other Indian writers on sex and love through the Middle Ages, and came to be seen as a foundational authority on sexuality. It also had a deep impact on Indian literature: on Sanskrit and vernacular erotic poetry, as in the fabulous eroticism of Kalidasa's *Kumarasambhava*, which devotes the whole of its eighth book to the love-making of Shiva and Parvati as a paradigm of the way lovers grow in knowledge of each other through sex. As a text that was very aware of theorists on psychology and sex, this book echoes some of the concerns of *The Kama Sutra*, and was criticized by some Indians in later ages for its too overt sexuality.

The cataloguing of behaviour, acts, moods and traits is a cultural obsession in India, and the way the book is organized reflects that numbers game: the sixty-four sexual positions, for example, echo the sixty-four diseases in medical texts, the sixty-four arts, and even the sixty-four 'playful games' of Shiva. The book itself is wrapped in a further numerical conceit – that it is only

him (with pardonable enthusiasm, as he benefited greatly from the king's patronage) as 'virtuous and patriotic; all people celebrate his praises in song'. The king's life story is told by his chief minister, Bhanna, in the first full-scale Indian secular biography, which begins with the drama of his accession, the younger brother of the murdered king 'whose royal appearance and demeanour', as the Chinese monk also says, 'were recognized in conjunction with his great military talents. His qualifications moved heaven and earth; his sense of justice was admired by gods and men.' After Harsha 'made himself master of India, his renown spread abroad everywhere, and all his subjects reverenced his virtues. The empire having gained stability, the people were at peace.'

What followed immediately taps into old themes in Indian history, suggesting no one more than Ashoka himself. Once peace was established, says Hsuan Tsang, 'Harsha put an end to offensive military expeditions, and began to put into storage all his weaponry. He gave himself up to religious duties and prohibited the slaughter of animals ... he founded *sangharamas* (Buddhist monasteries) wherever there were sacred traces of religion.' But as with earlier epochs, the king's role in religion was ecumenical, and there was no state religion. Instead religious festivals embraced all faiths in great acts of royal charity. 'Every fifth year,' says Hsuan Tsang, 'Harsha convoked a grand assembly and distributed the surplus of his royal stores as an act of charity.' In 642 Hsuan Tsang witnessed a great gathering of this kind on the sands at the confluence of the Ganges and the Jumna, where 'from ancient times until now, royal and noble personages endowed with virtue and love, for distribution of their charitable offerings, have all come to this place for that purpose. At the present time King Harsha, following this custom, has distributed here the accumulated wealth of five years, over a period of seventy-five days.' This, as we saw in Chapter 2, may be the 'great assembly' mentioned by the Greeks in 300 BC, and the predecessor perhaps of the medieval and modern festival at the same place, the *Kumbh Mela*, the biggest religious gathering on Earth. However, like a number of other present-day traditions – including the *ramlilas* in Benares and the *durga puja* in Calcutta – the *kumbh* reached its present form during the British period.

Harsha would be remembered among Buddhists as the fourth and last pillar of Buddhism, after Ashoka, the Greek king Menander and Kanishka, and the intellectual exchanges in his day between India and China are part of the history of the whole of humanity. Hsuan Tsang returned to China in 646. The Wild Goose Pagoda built to store his manuscripts still stands in Xian, and the small monastery that is his final resting place survives in a delectable wooded valley outside the city. Spared at the express command of the communist leader Chou En-lai (or so its abbot told me many years back), its library still holds palm-leaf manuscripts in the Pali language of Sri Lanka.

A stele in the library shows Hsuan Tsang, rucksack on his back, a lamp to light his way, braving the elements to bring home his precious cargo of manuscripts. Only fairly recently, copies of his letters have come to light, written nearly twenty years on to his old friends in India: they are among the most arresting texts in the history of civilization. To the master of Maghagda he sends news from China: 'the great king of the Tang, with the compassion of a chakravarti-raja, rules in tranquillity and spreads the teachings of the Buddha: he has even penned with his own hand a preface to a translation he ordered copied and circulated, and it is being studied too by neighbouring countries.' To the abbot of Mahbodhi in Bodhgaya the tone is even more touching, for they belonged to opposed schools:

> It has been a long time now since we parted, which has only increased
> my admiration for you … Now there is a messenger returning to India,
> I send you my sincere regards and a little memento as a token of my
> gratitude. It is too inadequate to express my deep feelings for you.
> I hope you appreciate that. When I was returning from India I lost a
> horse-load of manuscripts in the river Indus. I attach herewith my list
> and request that copies be sent to me. This much for the present.
> Yours, the monk Hsuan Tsang

The coming of Islam

The synchronicities of history are sometimes striking. In the summer of 632 Hsuan Tsang, on the last stage of his journey to seek the wisdom of India, was staying in Kashmir, then a land of hundreds of Buddhist monasteries. At that point Buddhism, having spread to China, the Far East and Southeast Asia, may well have had the largest number of followers of any organized religion in the world. That June, far away to the west in Medina, the Prophet Muhammad died, having enjoined his followers to 'seek knowledge as far as China'. An amazing new epoch in the history of the world was about to open up – one that would see within a single century the establishment of an Islamic caliphate and the spread of Islam over a vast area from Spain to the Indus valley.

The coming of Islam is fraught with difficulty in Indian historiography, and all the more so in light of the confrontational rhetoric of international politics at this moment in the twenty-first century. It is the subject of two great and conflicting narratives that have long been articulated in Indian politics, culture and education. On the one hand there is the secular interpretation fostered, for example, by the Congress Party, the main force in the Independence movement, which is supported by many secular Indians, by many Muslims, and by many liberal progressive

Hindus. On the other hand there is the religious interpretation, broadly espoused by Hindu nationalists of various persuasions, from hardline fundamentalists to many in the middle of the road, such as those who resented the partial communal politics bequeathed by the British. The first admits a tale of conquest, but one in which the foreign invaders adapted, changed and became Indian; in which conversion, more often than not, happened through dialogue, and out of which an extraordinary exchange and interaction developed over many centuries, during which northern India became an Indo-Islamic civilization in which most Hindus and Muslims coexisted peacefully: in other words, another phase of India's unity in diversity. The Hindu nationalist view, however, says that the coming of Islam marked a break, an alien intrusion; it insists that foreign dynasties came bearing a form of monotheism fundamentally irreconcilable with Hindu religion, and that their intolerance towards Indian religions began centuries of hostility exacerbated in the modern era by British 'divide and rule' tactics.

As always in history, both narratives are to an extent true; yet both are distortions of much more complex realities that differed on the ground in every region. But both these narratives coexist in the minds of most Indian people, and one or other tends to come to the fore in times of peace or times of stress, especially when fomented by unscrupulous politicians for electoral gain. Certain historical facts, though, are insurmountable, the foremost being the Partition of the subcontinent on religious lines in 1947, which, however we argue, was a fundamental break with India's past. The roots of these events lay far back in history.

At the centre of the Old World, India had long had cultural and linguistic connections with the West and central Asia. Now Arabs, Turks, Afghans and Mongols enter the story in a new age of migrations. Islam seems to have first reached the coast of Kerala with Arab traders in the seventh century, and the earliest mosque on the subcontinent is said to be the one at Cranganore, the successor to the old Roman settlement of Muziris. In the south the migrants came peacefully, and over time became thoroughly acculturized. A military attack on Sind from the Indus delta in 711 led to Muslim settlement in parts of what is now southern Pakistan; but as late as the 980s a Persian geographer using first-hand merchants' reports could describe, for example, Lahore, in the heart of the Pakistani Punjab, as a purely Hindu city 'full of bazaars and idol temples', a city whose people were 'entirely infidels, with no Muslims'. It was not until the early eleventh century that Turkic and Afghan armies bearing the faith of Islam began to make headway against the Hindu kingdoms of northern India. These military incursions of Islamic conquerors in the Middle Ages influenced the cultures of the north forever, an intensely dramatic tale that brought about one of the biggest stories of cultural cross-over in history. One concomitant, for example, was the conversion of huge numbers of Indians to Islam. This phenomenon is not yet satisfactorily explained by historians; no doubt it was partly through coercion, but in part too a reaction to the hierarchical and oppressive nature of Brahminical religion in many places towards the lower castes, and, a response to the democratic bent of Islam. But this great historical movement began with violence.

Mahmud of Ghazni

Ghazni, eastern Afghanistan. Clouds of dust swirl around the crumbling citadel and the scorching blast of summer rises from the arid Afghan plateau. 'A truly miserable place,' the Mughal Babur wrote. 'Why kings who hold Hindustan and Khurasan [Persia] would ever make such a wretched place their capital has always been a source of amazement to me.' A few hours south of Kabul on the road to Kandahar, this was the capital of a vast Muslim empire in the eleventh century. The security advice these days is to stay only a short time. At the tomb of Sultan Mahmud, a plain stone slab with swirls of Kufic lettering, a knot of old, turbaned Afghans are at prayer. Mahmud is still remembered here as presiding over a high tide of Islam.

recorded on bronze images commissioned by Rajaraja's sister Kundavi. After all this, his uncle, rather than the boy-prince, succeeded to the throne (shades of *Hamlet* or *The Lion King*?), and is regarded by some Tamil historians, though not all, as a 'wicked uncle'. Although Rajaraja was 'begged by the people to become king and dispel the darkness of the Kali age', he refused to do so. 'He did not desire the kingdom for himself, even inwardly, so long as his uncle coveted the rule of the land …' The tale no doubt conceals infighting within the royal house, as seems to have happened with so many ancient and medieval Indian successions. But to placate court factions, and after 'certain marks were observed on his body … showing that he was the very Vishnu descended to Earth', (which has hints of the Rama story) his uncle named Rajaraja as his heir. So he was installed as crown prince, while the uncle himself 'bore the burden of ruling the Earth'.

With the self-possession of Rama in exile, the young prince did not fight, but waited for his time to come. When it finally did, the king displayed a practical genius, a ruthlessness and a knack for self-promotion that has left an enduring mark on the cultural, political and religious life of southern India.

Rajaraja's personal deity – his family god (*kulandeva*) as the Tamils put it – was Shiva, but as with all great Indian rulers he was an enthusiastic patron of other faiths, building a temple and a huge Buddhist monastery in Nagapattinam, the main seaport, to welcome Eastern pilgrims. (This, incidentally, continued to be used by Asian pilgrims into the sixteenth century, and was not demolished until the 1860s.) He even sanctioned Buddhist sculptures on the walls of his great Shiva temple in Tanjore, built to commemorate his rulership, his conquests and, above all, himself.

Rajaraja's temple at Tanjore is a World Heritage Site today, but still a living shrine. The weathered red sandstone *gopuras*, or gate towers, announce the ceremonial entrance, looking for all the world like exotic petrified vegetation with their sprouting ornaments and horned finials. The temple is named after the great king, Rajarajesvaram (Lord of Rajaraja), and has lengthy inscriptions about his victories and donations carved all around its walls. The royal family and courtiers emulated his generosity by making lavish gifts of bronzes, utensils, candelabra and furnishings. Most prominent among the donors, though, are not his ten queens, but his 'beloved elder sister' Kundavi, with whom he seems to have had an unusually intense relationship. She takes priority over her brother's queens in all the inscriptions, and he would later marry one of her daughters and name one of his own daughters after her.

The great gateways open on to a campus so elegant and spacious after the crowded hurly-burly of the town that the effect is eye-popping. It measures 1200 × 800 feet and is entirely surrounded by a pillared cloister, with a dado and pilasters, that runs along a magnificent granite wall 40 feet high. Its beautiful and austere

classicism is enlivened by rows of little sculpted figures of Nandi, Shiva's bull, along the top. Peeping over the wall, the bending heads of cocoa palms are tousled beguilingly by the warm wind as knots of pilgrims make their way around the shrines in brilliant saris of lemon, crimson and gold.

The court was a great ritual space, a theatre for royal ceremonies. There are perhaps few places in the world where so old a building is still perfectly preserved, and still works as a living institution. In the centre of the courtyard the main shrine stands on a great platform, with a huge pyramidal vimana (tower) 216 feet high, which, when it was completed in 1010, was the tallest building in India. The completion was celebrated in a grand festival in which the top royal acting troupe performed a specially written musical play telling the story of the king and his temple. Sadly, the text is now lost, though sitting in the courtyard in brilliant sunshine, with today's festival tents flapping, it is pleasing to imagine Rajaraja as prince and script editor-in-chief – both Hal and Hamlet, solid and quicksilver, swordsman and poet-philosopher – giving his actors last-minute instructions on how to deliver their lines extolling him: '… his deeds such as to make the goddess of fortune his own wife, and the goddess of the great Earth, his mistress.'

generally share in the surplus they generated, but still their culture had many qualities, and one notable area was pluralism in religion. Intolerance, of course, is the monopoly of no civilization, and it is easy to find examples of Hindu kings showing fanatical intolerance to Buddhists and Jains in the Middle Ages, and even towards other Hindu sects. But if a broad tendency can be detected, it is perhaps that foreign dynasties eschewed state religion altogether, and though some native dynasties favoured one – the Mauryans with Jainism or Buddhism, for example, the Guptas with Vaishnavaism, the Cholas with Saivism – enlightened Indian rulers were still active supporters of other faiths. The key, if at all possible, was pluralism.

In the south the old native kingdoms went their own way until the early fourteenth century, untroubled by the wider world. In the north the great powers of the late antique period and early Middle Ages were buffeted by blows through the eleventh and twelfth centuries until the establishment of the Delhi sultanate in 1192 began the centuries-long domination of Afghan, Turkic and Mughal dynasties, some of whose kings aggressively propagated Islam. But, as we shall see, accommodation came. In a telling anecdote that could be multiplied over and over, the great traveller ibn Battuta tells how, in the 1330s, even the temples at Khajuraho, with their magically erotic sculpture illustrating the cosmic marriage of Shiva and Parvati, became a source for Muslim holy men as well as Hindus. All of them were united in that perennial Indian quest – seeking after wisdom.

As for the Rama story with which I began, in the Middle Ages it became a metaphor, a carrier of meaning for the Indian experience, a lens by which to see the shifting currents of Indian history. There are said to be more than 300 versions, some containing radical retellings, in Tamil, for example, in Marathi, Telugu and Bengali, and in the northern lingua franca, Hindi. There is a Muslim Rama story told by the Mopylas, the old boat-building caste of Kerala: a tale of 'Sultan Ram' set firmly in tropical southern India in a Muslim milieu. There is even a Tamil 'Life of the Prophet' modelled on the Tamil *Ramayana*. In such ways the tale became a vision of Indian history: another root of a shared past, available to all communities and even all religions. Like all great creations of India, it came to belong everywhere. As an eminent member of India's Supreme Court, a Muslim, puts it:

> The entire country is Ramjanmabhumi, the birth land of Rama. The
> Ramjanmasthan, the birthplace, lies, however, in the hearts and minds
> of all those who have, over the centuries, loved, respected and wor-
> shipped Shri Rama as Maryada Purshottram: an ideal of rectitude,
> integrity, decency and sheer humanity.

OPPOSITE

Tiruvannamalai: fabulous images from the Kartikai *festival. This ancient Tamil hill shrine is celebrated by the 7th-century saints, and was later enriched by Rajaraja himself.*

5
The Rule of Reason: The Great Mughals

AT THE GREAT FORT Bala Hissar the trees are shaken by the north wind that blows through spring and summer across the Kabul plain. Zigzagging over bare brown hills, the city walls of Kabul were first built to withstand the attacks of the Huns in the fifth century. Kabul has seen many attackers since then – Genghis Khan, Tamburlaine, Mughals, Persians, British – and they are still at war today, as the fighting spreads in Helmand province. But here in the early sixteenth century a new invasion of India was

planned, which would have a profound effect on the history of the subcontinent.

When I was here in the mid-1990s, during the first war with the Taliban, the city had been devastated: there was no electricity, no street lighting; at night the occasional car's headlights swept through the jagged pinnacles and murky shadows of a broken city. Since the overthrow of the Taliban in 2001, international commerce has returned and new buildings are going up everywhere, despite the rumble of war in the south. But the incessant fighting over the last quarter century has also brought a vast expansion of the population, spreading shanties up the hillsides, draping dingy suburbs over what was in the late 1960s, as all old Afghan hands will tell you, a heavenly land: as the poet Peter Levi put it, 'the light garden of the angel king'.

Babur, the first Mughal

The tomb of Babur, founder of the Mughal dynasty that ruled northern India from 1526 to 1857, lies in a once-lovely valley a short walk from the city centre – a walk that opens up views of the diversity of Afghan history. It is easy today to think of Afghanistan as a hotbed of Islamic fundamentalism, but traces of another, richer history are all around us. This place is a witness to the waves of history on the subcontinent, for Afghanistan, as we have already seen, has always been part of that story. In the Late Bronze Age and after, the Kabul valley was one of the lands of the Rig-Veda. It was a great centre of Buddhist culture in the early centuries AD, and was ruled by Hindu shahs between 600 and the tenth century AD. Indeed, until the civil war of the 1980s and the Russian invasion it still had a big Hindu population, nearly a quarter of a million strong, mainly traders, craftsmen, practitioners of traditional 'Yunani' (Graeco-Roman) medicine. Now only a few hundred families are left, but the valley bears evidence of its multi-faith past, when Hindus, Buddhists and Muslims came here to worship. There are the remains of a Kushan stupa at the southern end of the valley; an old Muslim cemetery commemorates the first Islamic missionaries to Kabul in the seventh century AD; and there was a Hindu temple still in this area until the Russian invasion. Sadly, the old picnics in the groves of mulberries are a thing of the past – at least for now.

But the most evocative spot of all is the garden of Babur, burial place of the legendary Mughal leader. His was an amazing tale. Born in Fergana, proclaimed king in the Tajik city of Khodzent, he was a direct descendant of Genghis Khan and Tamburlaine. He conquered Kabul in 1504, and it was from here that he launched his final attack on India in 1525, which at that time was, paradoxically, ruled by the Lodi sultans who had originally come from Afghanistan. Babur's bold and risky adventure succeeded. He founded the Mughal dynasty, whose leaders would become among the greatest and most glamorous rulers in the world. But he never forgot Kabul. In his memoirs he complains about the hot, dusty climate of India ('a place with few attractions … and no good melons'). Kabul was the place he really loved, 'with its excellent climate, overlooking the great lake, and three meadows that look very beautiful when the plains are green'. He liked the valley in particular, his home for twenty years, its altitude giving it the perfect summer climate, a place where vines, olive trees and fruit orchards could thrive. The garden here was laid out between 1504 and 1528, and has been popular with the people of the city ever since. The inscription on the tomb is his: 'If there is a paradise on Earth, this is it, this is it, this is it!'

Babur tells us that he felt most at home in these rugged landscapes with their emerald green valleys and fruit orchards; their brown whalebacks of mountains streaked with snow; in the serais and bazaars of Bukhara Merv and Samarkand. He never mastered an Indian language, but spoke the Chaghtai dialect of Turkic from Mughalistan, the lands north of the Syr Darya river stretching towards Lake Balkash. And to the end, in the sweltering plains of India, he still hankered after the

The tomb of Babur
today, outside Kabul.

wide skies of central Asia, the purple deserts of Samarkand dotted with flowers after the spring rains.

Forty years ago, in the days of the 'Hippy Trail', this was still a delightful spot, with magnificent chinar trees and the scent of wild rose and jasmine in the air. Since then the catastrophe for Afghanistan has also swept up even the greatest Muslim monuments. Decades of neglect, twenty-five years of war, and several years of drought have dried up watercourses and killed all the trees and plants, leaving it derelict and engulfed by the urban sprawl of shanties. Now it is being restored: the gardens are to be replanted with trees and flowers, so it may once again be the haven it was in Mughal times. Like so much of the tragedy of Afghanistan over the last three decades, from the destruction of the Bamiyan Buddhas to the wrecking of the Kabul Museum, the battle is also against the loss of the past.

But the garden is not just a setting for this part of the story of India; it is also a symbol of a civilization that we have come to view as quintessentially Indian. It was the first of the Mughal gardens of the subcontinent, while the garden at Dholpur, south of Agra, was almost Babur's first act of state in India. Others laid out by his successors include the magnificent group of gardens at Srinagar, overlooking the Dal Lake in Kashmir and now languishing unvisited under the shadow of the jihadists; and the recently rediscovered Moonlit Garden over the Jumna from the Taj Mahal. The Kabul garden was the first model. Babur laid

As for Nasukh melons, 'yellow skin soft as glove leather, they are amazingly delicious, there is nothing like them'. Babur records his own foibles, his illnesses, boils and abcesses, his excessive drinking; he is a human personality. As a leader and man of action, he was also peremptory in his cruelty. A typical passage reads: 'I ordered the cook to be flayed alive, the taster cut to pieces, one of the women trampled by elephants, the other shot.'

Babur describes a gripping scene at Delhi after the great victory. There were signs of disaffection in the army, reminiscent of Alexander the Great at the river Beas. Deaths through sickness and heat were increasing, and so was hatred of India and nostalgia for the Kabuli gardens. 'Many began to sicken and die, as if under a pestilential wind. That's why most of the great warriors and chiefs began to lose heart.' Unwilling to stay in Hindustan they began to leave. This was a key moment.

> ... if aged and experienced leaders say such things, it is no fault, for
> such men have enough sense and intelligence to distinguish between
> prudence and imprudence and to discern good from evil after a
> decision has been made. Such a person considers everything for
> himself and he knows that when something has been decided there is
> no sense in endlessly repeating words that have already been spoken.
> But these were men that I expected if I went through fire or water,
> they would go in with me and emerge with me and be at my side
> wherever I went, not speak out against me.

So Babur speaks to the council just as his Spanish contemporary Francisco Pizarro did to his men in South America, both being conscious that a continent lay before them that would be won by those who were prepared to gamble all. His message to his commanders standing in the mid-May heat of the northern Indian plain was direct:

> I said rule and conquest do not come without tools and conquest.
> Kingship and princehood are not possible without liegemen and
> domains. For some years we have gone through hardships, traversed
> long distances, cast ourselves and our soldiers into the dangers of war
> and battle. Through God's grace we have defeated such numerous
> enemies and taken such vast realms. Why throw it all away now, after
> gaining it at such cost? Shall we go back to Kabul and stay poor?

They went on, most of them, though Babur never lost his longing for his old homeland. His descendants for a long time would nurse imperial dreams of their central Asian homeland: they even, unwisely, fought battles there. But eventually their ancestral lands around Fergana would become a distant memory; the orchards of Samarkand, the legendary Timurid capital, once so ardently desired, would become a forsaken passion. Babur's descendants became Indian.

The legacy of Babur

Babur, like Tamburlaine and the Tuqluqs, was an invader, and his career was driven by violence. In the sacred writings of the Sikhs, Guru Nanak says he was a messenger of death, who 'terrified Hindustan', and accuses his armies of the rape of Hindu women. Mughal sources, on the other hand, say he went out of his way to protect the civilian population in war, even compensating farmers if their crops were ruined. But he was a man of his time, and his was a time when striking fear was part of being a king. There is much argument about his legacy now, especially by Hindu nationalists, who see the Mughal as an enemy of India. And it is true that he could on occasion talk the language of jihad, though only perhaps when his army seemed to be losing its nerve.

Also, as the Koran enjoins, he could be merciless towards unbelievers when they resisted him. But did he destroy Hindu temples, as others had done in the past and would in the future? Whether the mosque in Ayodhia was built on top of a destroyed Hindu temple has never been shown, but conquerors did this sort of thing, and whether Babur was different we cannot say. His bloodthirsty description of the killing of infidels at the siege of Chanderi in 1528, with the mass suicide of hundreds more (who 'went to hell') is a case in point. He was hardly squeamish about killing unbelievers, just as Akbar the Great could kill 'idolaters' and leave pillars made of their skulls. Such things, I daresay, were typical of wars of the time; if a city resisted, punishment was often merciless. But Babur was an intelligent man and saw that conciliation of enemies was the path

BELOW
Babur and his son Humayun with their ancestor Tamburlaine, the 'world conqueror'. Small origins but pride in their lineage gave them a great sense of history.

Akbar the Great: 'In the past, to our shame, we forced many Hindus to adopt the faith of our ancestors. Now it has become clear to me that in our troubled world, so full of contradictions, it cannot be wisdom to assert the unique truth of one faith over another. The wise person makes justice his guide and learns from all. Perhaps in this way the door may be opened again, whose key has been lost.'

The Golden Temple at Amritsar. Despite initial conflicts with the Sikhs, Akbar granted them land on which to build their great shrine.

The tale of the Taj begins with the death of Shah Jahan's most beloved wife Mumtaz. In his grief he decided to create a wonderful and eternal monument to her, a tomb to represent on Earth the house of the queen in paradise. For the location Jahan went to some lengths to acquire a plot by the river Jumna from the Hindu rajah of Amber, to whom he gave four mansions in Agra as payment. We will see shortly why the specific landscape was so important to his plan. When work began in 1632 one of the builders' very first jobs was to plant trees so that they would have grown to some height by the time the building was ready more than ten years later.

One might think it hardly possible to say anything new about one of the best-known buildings in the world. But fascinating new theories about its conception have emerged only recently. The plan of the Taj was influenced in the first place by earlier Mughal ideas about gardens, especially the Eight Paradises Pavilion, which is the funerary form of a paradise garden. This had many ancient relatives in the Byzantine and classical Mediterranean world, and even in the ancient Near East. But the plan also drew on number symbolism in Hindu and Buddhist thought. These numerical schemes were assimilated by the architects into Islamic traditions about paradise. In medieval Muslim tradition paradise had at least seven levels, often eight. In particular, the famous mystic ibn Arabi in his *Meccan Revelations* of *c.*1230 described paradise as three gardens, of which the third is divided into eight sections with eight doors. These ideas of a paradise pavilion had long been present in Mughal art – they are used in the tomb of Humayun in Delhi – and, interestingly enough, Renaissance artists such as Bramante, Michelangelo and Palladio were also interested in this numerical symbolism.

To this architectural plan Jahan's architects added the largest scriptural inscriptional programme in the Islamic world: twenty-five quotations from the Koran, including fourteen complete suras (chapters), were depicted on the great gate, the mausoleum and the mosque in elegant black marble inlay on rectangular white marble plaques framed by red sandstone bands and enlivened by ornate floral patterns above the gate arches. The theme of the inscriptions connects with the function of the building as a tomb. It was eschatological, that is to say, concerned with the Day of Judgement. All the suras on the building speak about the Day of Judgement, divine mercy and the paradise promised to the faithful. Indeed, one new theory about the Taj sees the building as a symbolic replica of the throne of God on Judgement Day, specifically as expressed in a mystical diagram drawn by ibn Arabi and reproduced in the manuscripts of his *Meccan Revelations*. This may be too schematic: but, nevertheless, as a whole the programme of the Taj represents a highly intellectual conception of the tomb as the house prepared for Mumtaz (and eventually Jahan himself) in paradise.

ABOVE, BELOW AND OPPOSITE

Mughal civilization. Above: Humayun's tomb. Right: Fatepur Sikri. Opposite: The palace at Agra.

6
Freedom and Liberation

I'M SITTING OUT ON THE TERRACE of a little boarding house in Allahabad, one of the last of the British bungalows that once gave the city – alternatively known as the 'Oxford of India' or the 'Oven of India' – its low-rise charm. Tea and fruit cake are on the table. The owners of the hotel are Parsees (key people here during the Raj, the time of British rule: the first photographers; the first car dealers; some of the first native lawyers, dentists and doctors, were all Parsees). They are related to

Feroz Gandhi, who married Jawaharlal Nehru's daughter Indira, whose family were also Allahabad people. The hotel has a rather faded touch of the Old World, but I prefer it to the new, slick international-style hotels in the Civil Lines (the former European city), despite the attraction of air-conditioned rooms, plush bars and wireless Internet. The front garden, with its old well and spreading pipal tree, is a nice place to sit after a long day and watch the crowds of lawyers, with their starched collars and gowns, hurrying to their waiting auto-rickshaws.

Allahabad ('Godville' is Mark Twain's apt translation) has already appeared several times in this story. It got its present name from the emperor Akbar, who proclaimed his new religion here in 1575 (see page 198). At the *sangam*, the sacred confluence of the Ganges and the Jumna, he built a giant fortress, one of the four greatest Mughal forts, along with Delhi, Agra and

PREVIOUS PAGES

Mumbai, Maximum City: embodiment of India's growth and a scene from the first war of Independence in 1857.

OPPOSITE

*Above: One of Felix
Beato's photographs of
the devastation wrought
in the Mutiny and its
aftermath. Below:
Outside Government
House in 1858 as the
East India Company's
rule came to an end.*

Lahore. What a role the place has played in Indian history! As the ancient Hindu holy site of Prayag, it hosts the *Kumbh Mela* festival, which on one night in 2001 attracted 25 million pilgrims, dwarfing all the other gatherings there have ever been on Earth. It is also the final point in the circuit of India's holy sites in the *Mahabharata*, and still known among Hindus as the 'King of Holy Places'. Inside the Mughal fort is the famous stone pillar carrying the decrees of Ashoka and the inscriptions of Samudragupta and Jahangir. The mythological navel of the Earth, it is a place whose symbolic life is almost richer than its real history.

When they became the rulers of India in the bloody aftermath of the Mutiny of 1857, the chastened British were mindful of these great associations. It was a few yards away from Ashoka's pillar, on the outer bastion, that Lord Canning proclaimed the end of the East India Company's rule and the beginning of Victoria's Raj (an event commemorated in the little garden of Minto Park as 'India's Magna Carta'). But that came after savagery. The Civil Lines, with their neat, tree-lined avenues, their parks, gymkhana clubs and orderly cantonments, were laid out over eight Indian villages that were razed to the ground in revenge, and where 'nigger' women and children perished along with the 'vilest malefactors'.

In the next three decades the city fittingly became a centre of the nascent freedom movement. The site of British India's most important High Court, Allahabad was a city of lawyers, and the men who made India free, including Jawaharlal Nehru, the first prime minister, would all be British-educated lawyers. The Nehrus, old Kashmiri Brahmins, were Allahabad people, and the house owned by Nehru's father, Motilal, still stands in the European town: a spacious estate, fitting for a rich advocate who became a London QC. Around it there are still many places with British associations: the university with its Gothic cloisters; the beautiful Anglican cathedral, all flying buttresses and stained glass; the Civil Lines shopping arcade, with Wheelers Bookshop and the neoclassical Picture Palace; not forgetting Barnetts House of Confectionery (now the Harsh Hotel), which serviced the Imperial Airways stopover from Croydon to Calcutta. In Motilal's day a soon-to-be iconic Raj figure, the writer Rudyard Kipling, worked here for the local English-language newspaper, the *Pioneer*, which 'ably opposed Indian aspirations', as John Murray's *Guidebook* blithely put it. The *Pioneer* has long since moved to Lucknow, and the old newspaper building, another red-brick bungalow only yards from the Nehru residence, has been demolished since I was here in the summer of 2006, a victim of Allahabad's building boom. But the house where Kipling lodged is still here, in an overgrown garden inhabited by a bony cow and a mongoose. It is now lived in by a sprightly eighty-year-old journalist called Durga, who started with All India Radio in 1943, and covered the last phase of the freedom struggle. 'I was glad to see the back of the British,' she told me with a clear eye. 'Which people doesn't want to be free?'

Sitting here in Allahabad (a town I feel I know better than many in England), I am painfully conscious of my own ancestry. I am a child of post-war Britain, and though I could not see it at the time, colonialism shaped me too. In the 1950s and 1960s we were brought up at home and school with rose-tinted spectacles about the British Empire. Scented with saddle soap and railway steam, and orchestrated by Edward Elgar, we were given a Raj drenched in nostalgia in novels, on television and in the cinema. But, however we dress it up, imperialism is still imperialism. India was turned into a classic colonial economy, exporting raw materials and importing finished goods. The natural resources of India were plundered, and her people treated like children by those who saw themselves as the superior race. These days some British historians put forward the argument that colonialism was a good thing, lighting the world's path to progress. I have to say that I am not, by and large, of that persuasion. Over thirty-five years travelling in Asia, Africa and the Americas, seeing things on the ground, has given me a different perspective, and has left me with the conviction that its impact has been largely destructive. The age of European empires unleashed tremendous historical forces, many of them no doubt creative, but for much of the population of the globe this was a cataclysmic epoch that left few native cultures intact. Only great and resilient civilizations, such as India, were able to hold their own, take what was useful, and emerge still themselves.

The period of the British Raj – from the East India Company's rise to power in the eighteenth century to Independence in 1947 – lasted roughly 200 years, a time comparable to the Kushan era, but shorter than the Mughals'. It is a long and tortured story, full of splendours and miseries, of pride and greed, and of fantastic cultural crossovers, as remarkable (I am tempted to say more so) than even under the Mughals. In the open-minded atmosphere of the eighteenth century there were many meetings of minds. General Charles 'Hindoo' Stuart in Calcutta bathed daily in the Ganges, recommended English ladies to wear the sari, and made the first collection of Indian art. With striking foresight, Stuart also argued for native customs to be allowed in sepoy army regiments. In his *Vindication of the Hindoos* he scathingly deprecated European missionaries and praised Hinduism as a religion that 'little needs the meliorating hand of Christianity to render its votaries a sufficiently correct and moral people for all the useful purposes of a civilized society'.

Such 'White Mughals' had their counter-
parts in the intellectual sciences. William Jones
(see page 37), James Prinsep and Francis
Buchanan, for example, were leading lights in
the rediscovery of ancient Indian history; nor
should one forget the remarkable Warren
Hastings, the troubled first governor general of
British India, who knew native languages and
played an instrumental role in the cultivation of
scholarship in Bengal. This meeting of cultures
led to a prodigious multilingual flowering of
Bengali civilization that would eventually bring
the Bengali reformer and polymath Ram Roy
sailing into Liverpool in 1833 on his own
version of the search for the 'meeting place of
the oceans.' Orientalism these days has become
an overused and overstated catch-all. Colonial
forms of knowledge could indeed be instrum-
ents of oppression, but between the late eighteenth and early twentieth centuries England
and Bengal would engage in one of history's
great cross-cultural exchanges, and one that is
by no means exhausted yet.

But the British relationship with India did
not develop further on those lines. In the end,
the ideologies and exigencies of empire proved
too strong. If one by-product of the eighteenth
century was a love affair, the nineteenth century
saw the falling apart, and the twentieth century the tragic and costly divorce.
Thankfully, in our own time the children and grandchildren are friends and are
building a new relationship.

ABOVE

*Warren Hastings, first
governor general of
British India. A major
figure in the British
'discovery' of the Indian
past, Hastings is a
problematical figure due
a re-evaluation.*

The East India Company and the 1857 rebellion

The story of the East India Company uncannily echoes that of modern multi-
national companies, who trade in natural resources and gain new spheres of
influence through economic intervention, private armies and proxy war. The
British triumphed because of India's own internal divisions, the decline of
Mughal power in the north and because they controlled the sea. Where earlier

ABOVE

*Clive receiving the
diwan of Bengal in
1765, the moment the
British moved from trade
to real power.*

conquerors had entered India through the Khyber and the Northwest Frontier, the British extended their influence along her coasts, founding fortified trading ports in Calcutta, Madras and Bombay as the first bases of their rule. They were backed by armed force, though at first the numbers were small: 2200 Europeans and a similar number of native troops won the decisive battle at Plassey in Bengal in 1757 against the last independent nawab of Bengal, who also had a tiny force from the French East India Company. A similarly sized army gained victory at Wandiwash in the south, where, between the 1740s and 1760s, the British and the French fought out another part of their global confrontation. Then, in 1765, the Mughal Shah Alam in Delhi formally awarded the British the *diwan* of Bengal – that is, the right to raise revenues. What had begun as a speculative piece of Elizabethan merchant-venturing had entered a new phase.

In the south too the struggle with the French soon reached its climax. Between the 1760s and 1799 the British fought four wars with the Muslim

The coming-on of the MONSOONS;— or —The Retreat from SERINGAPATAM.

LEFT

Political cartoon of the day by Gillray showing the British in retreat from Seringapatam in 1791. The British would come back with a vengeance.

rulers of Mysore, who were French allies, ending in the siege of the island fortress of Seringapatam in 1799, in which Sultan Tipu was killed. At that battle the armed forces at the disposal of the Company were 50,000 strong, the size of a big European army. Investment now grew, and in the next few years Company profits rose astronomically: accounts registered with the British parliament show that revenues rose from over £8 million in 1794 to £13.5 million in 1803 – the equivalent of three-quarters of a billion today. The changing perspective is revealed in the vast archive of the Company now preserved in the British Library. In the aftermath of the victory over Tipu the governor general, Richard Wellesley (brother of the future victor of Waterloo), wrote:

> Seringapatam I shall retain full sovereignty for the Company as being a Tower of Strength from which we may at any time shake Hindostan to its centre, if any combination should ever be formed against our interests. I shall not at present enlarge upon the advantages which are likely to be derived to the British interests from this settlement, they are too obvious to require any detailed explanation.

Soon India could be depicted in British art as a naked black female, submissively offering her riches to Britannia. The conquest had happened piecemeal and opportunistically, with no thought-out, long-term goal. It was effected at no expense to the British taxpayer, by mercenaries picking off regional threats one by one. By the 1830s the Company archives reveal a shift from trade in textiles to ownership of land, and at this point the colonial project acquires a new ideological tone that is exemplified in Lord Macaulay's 1835 edict on Indian education, which announced the replacement of Persian by English as the new language of government. With this there also came a new emphasis on the desirability of spreading the Christian religion. From now on British dominion in India was not only to be about making money, but about changing India.

These interventionist attitudes, with their increasingly strident Christian tone, form the background to the 1857 Mutiny, the greatest rising against any colonial power in the Age of Empire. The rising began as a protest in the army ranks against British insensitivity to Hindu religious custom, but rapidly spread as a rebellion against foreign rule in which even Muslim jihadists for the moment made common cause with Hindus. As rebellion spread like wildfire up and down the Grand Trunk Road from Bengal to the Punjab, the presence of Britain in India hung in the balance. But in the end, by luck and grit and ruthlessness, the British gained the upper hand. The war was conducted with horrific violence and savage reprisals by both sides. Both Hindu and Muslim rebels expressed their loyalty to the ageing Mughal in Delhi, Shah Bahadur, who, after the defeat, was exiled to Burma. His sons were killed in cold blood by the British, who were merciless in their revenge.

In their many colourful histories of the war the British retrospectively painted the rising as if it had come out of the blue, but there had in fact been many revolts against them over the previous fifty years, notably the Vellore Mutiny of 1806, in which southern rebels had proclaimed a son of Sultan Tipu as king. The rising of 1857 wrecked Mughal Delhi and its refined cultural life, and brought devastation on its population, many of whose adult males were summarily massacred. But the rising was a terrible shock to the British establishment, and it put an end to the 258-year existence of the Company. In the aftermath the British parliament decided to take direct control of its Indian possessions. Ever mindful of tradition, the first viceroy, Lord Canning, read Queen Victoria's proclamation on 1 November 1858 from the outer rampart of Akbar's fort at Allahabad, overlooking the sacred confluence. India was now to be taught the new secular dharma of the West.

LEFT

Shah Bahadur, the last Mughal. Focus of the rebels' patriotism in the Mutiny of 1857, he was banished to Burma where his tomb is now a place of prayer.

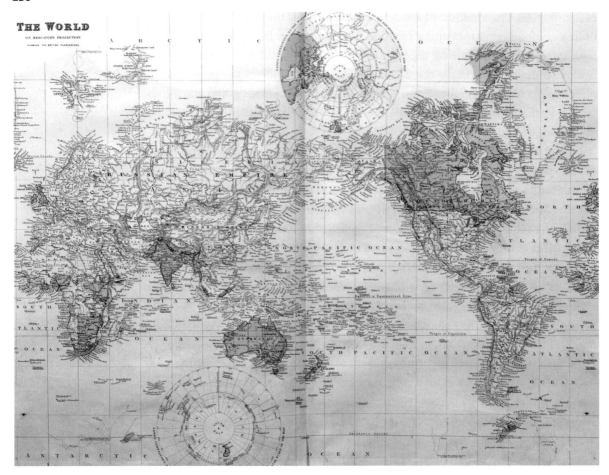

THE WORLD

ON MERCATOR'S PROJECTION

The British Empire on which the sun proverbially never set. But the British trade network stood or fell by their possession of India.

The strong perception far back in time, then, is of a broad cultural unity. The British would make their own vital contribution to this. Look at any map of India in the British handbooks of the Raj, and you will see pink covering the lands from Burma to Baluchistan and from Bhutan to Kerala, bounded by the natural frontiers of the sea, the Khyber, the Himalayas and the eastern jungles. Within the map, though, is the image of one of the most ingenious and adaptive empires in history, an immense patchwork loosely embracing almost a quarter of the population of the planet. In different colours are an amazing 675 feudatory and independent princely states (of whom seventy-three were ruled by rajas 'entitled to salutes of eleven guns or more'). Two of them, Hyderabad and Kashmir, are each the size of a large European country. This was the British solution to the diversity of India: an incredible political sleight of hand. An arrangement so extraordinary that it is hard to believe that it actually existed on the ground rather than just in the mind. But it was India.

Jewel in the Crown

Astonishingly, even at the peak of their empire, the British were able to rule the most populous region on Earth with just 50,000 troops and a quarter of a million administrators. Most of the day-to-day working of the empire was done by Indians, so they depended entirely on Indian cooperation; and as soon as that was withdrawn, the story was over for an empire acquired, as it was said in a disingenuous British understatement, 'in a fit of absent-mindedness'. That moment came with Indian disillusionment after the First World War, in which a million Indians fought for the king emperor and 50,000 died, and was confirmed by the massacre of Sikh demonstrators at Amritsar in 1919, from which the Indian perception of British fair play, goodwill and justice never quite recovered.

This is not to deny the complex and profound legacy of the British: above all, the English language, but also English ideas of secular law, education and constitutional government, the first attempt comprehensively to solve one of

ABOVE

Cavalry of the Queens Own Regiment alongside native sepoy troups of an Indian prince. The regiment went out to India in 1857 to crush the so-called mutiny.

Mahatma Gandhi's freedom march to the sea: his espousal of non-violent resistance would inspire many freedom fighters of the modern era.

saw something of the famines at first hand, and was horrified not only by the terrible suffering, but by the often callous disregard of the British government in its reluctance or slowness to shift surplus from one part of the country to another; in some regions not touched by famine grain was even shipped abroad. In his government role Hume had had the chance talk to many prominent Indians, and he was the initial connecting link between some of them. For this he would be attacked by Tories in London, one of whom suggested he should be hanged as a traitor.

The Congress Party held its first meeting in Bombay in 1885, in the middle of a crucial decade for the mobilization of Indian public opinion, when the British lifted press restrictions and hundreds of new newspapers appeared, most of them in the vernacular languages. A very broad church of radicals, socialists Hindus, Muslims and secularists, Congress did not at first set itself overtly against British rule, but initially pushed for greater representation, and only gradually was transformed into a more radical movement with the ultimate goal of self-rule.

The story of the Indian freedom movement from 1885 to 1947 has generally been told to the outside world through the powerful and seductive narrative of the Congress. Even Hollywood has turned the myth into a worldwide cinema epic (Nehru and Gandhi are, after all, among the greatest and most interesting figures in modern history). But, as always in history, there were other trajectories that could have taken India, and perhaps could still, on a different path. Representation of the different religious communities would become a particularly thorny issue. In 1906 some Muslim members split from Congress to form the Muslim League (see page 237). Then, in 1907, Congress split into two halves: Gandhi's mentor Gopal Krishna Gokhale's 'moderate faction' and the 'hot or hardline faction' of Bal Gangadhar Tilak, who supported direct action to overthrow the British and went to prison for it. Extremists, nationalists, secularists, Hindus and Muslims: the effort of keeping all on one track in the end proved too much for the Congress leadership. But after the First World War Mohandas Gandhi (another British-educated lawyer) became the dominant figure, with his appeal to Hindu popular discourse and his espousal of the key idea of *ahimsa*, non-violence. Under Gandhi's influence, Congress became the first integrated mass organization in the country, bringing together millions of people by specifically working against caste differences, untouchability, poverty and religious and ethnic boundaries. Although predominantly Hindu, it had members from virtually every religion, ethnic group, economic class and linguistic group. By the 1930s Congress could claim to be the true representative of the Indian people, and under Nehru's presidency formally declared as its goal *poorna swaraj* – complete independence.

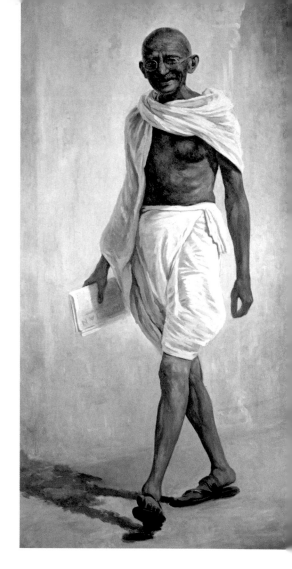

Partition: freedom but division

By the early 1930s it was obvious to most observers in Britain too that there was no way India could remain British, despite Churchill's blusterings and the rabid and racist polemics of the likes of Lord Rothermere and the right-wing British press. The issue then at stake was not whether India would be free, but what that India would be. The India beloved of Amir Khusro? The India made

The aftermath of the Calcutta Hindu–Muslim riots in 1946; the British army was caught in the middle. 'Quit India' said the graffiti.

patchwork reality by the British? An Indian federation of semi-autonomous states? Or a divided India? In the 1930s the united India that was the Congress dream was threatened by new developments that would have the greatest significance for India, but also impinge upon a wider world in the modern era.

Muslims made up nearly a quarter of British India. Their coreligionists, as we have seen, had been the rulers in the north for several centuries. But the British deposition of the last Mughal in 1858 had left them disinherited and fearful of the political power of a Hindu majority who had not always been well treated by their Muslim overlords. A new Islamic consciousness had already shown itself in the 1857 rebellion, and the future of Islam in a post-British India was already being canvassed in the radical *madrasahs* of Deoband. Back in 1900 the British had chosen to make the official language of India's most populous region, United Provinces, Hindi rather than Urdu, written in Devanagari, not Arabic, script. With this, many Muslims grew more and more concerned that in a future time they might be dominated by the Hindus who would 'suppress Muslim culture and religion'. One British official at the time reported to his masters that many Muslims saw their destinies as completely separate and

ABOVE

*Nehru (standing) and
Maulana Azad (seated
far left) in April 1942.*

thought that 'no fusion of the two communities was possible'. The great issue
that had preoccupied Akbar had returned to haunt India.

In response to these events, the Muslim League was founded in Dhaka in
1906, to represent Muslim interests in the forthcoming liberation struggle.
Among those who left Congress to join it was yet another British-educated
lawyer, Mohammed Ali Jinnah, a secular Shia who was destined to play a central
role in the history of modern India. Congress had always worked to draw
Muslims to its cause, but was often accused of being 'too Hindu', though some
eminent Muslims remained committed throughout to its secular goals,
including the philosopher, poet and educationalist Maulana Abul Kalam Azad,
who remained all his life a supporter of Hindu–Muslim unity and who was
the first minister of education in free India. In the end, events unfolded, as
they often do in history, partly by accident rather than design. The idea of
Muslim separatism was pushed first of all as a bargaining counter for seats in
parliament, then as a negotiation for autonomous Muslim states within a
federation; only later still did it become a serious demand for an independent
country.

It is a little-known paradox, though, that the idea of a separate country for Muslims was first mooted by a Hindu nationalist in 1924. At that time Jinnah and the Muslim League were still fighting for an Indian federation, with Muslims guaranteed a third of parliamentary seats. The fateful moment came in 1928, when Congress offered the League only a quarter of the seats. Compromise then would perhaps have changed the course of Indian history. For Jinnah, though, it was a 'parting of the ways'.

Whether Partition could or should have been avoided is a moot point that has been agonized over by many Indians and Pakistanis ever since. Indeed, from time to time one still reads articles in Indian newspapers that canvas the possibility of reunification. This is especially strongly argued by those who believe that Partition came about because of British realpolitik. Did the British tacitly approve it because it would help them divide and rule in the post-war, cold war world? Full publication of the papers in the last forty years at least absolves the British of that. Partition was really the result of multiple failures: the failure of Congress and the Muslim League to make concessions, and the failure of the British to act up to their historic responsibilities. The historical parallels are instructive. When the American states debated in 1776, the powerful ones conceded rights and powers to the small in order to achieve the Union. The goal of Congress was a united India, but in the end they were unable to make the concessions that would perhaps have got it. Jinnah, the brilliant but intractable Muslim leader, formerly a convinced nationalist, argued himself into a corner. The British, their power and sense of destiny broken by the Second World War, wearily gave up responsibility for their legacy and agreed to the Partition of India, separating the Muslim majority areas around the fringes of the subcontinent, including Sind and western Punjab, heartland of India's first civilization.

The British deadline for Independence was originally set for June 1948, but already Hindus and Muslims had clashed violently and bloodily in the northwest and Bengal. Beset by the growing threat of disorder, the British rushed the date forward to 14/15 August 1947. Fearing the reaction on the ground, the British didn't reveal the exact line of demarcation until the next day. In the Punjab the Sikhs who were divided by the line immediately took up arms to defend their own community. Meanwhile, Hindus and Muslims, often former neighbours, turned against each other amid rumour and hysteria. The result was terrible bloodshed and the largest migration in history, as 11 million people quit their ancestral villages and fled for their lives across the invisible border drawn up by a foreign power that was no longer present. The exact death toll will never be known; often estimated at one or two million, it may well have run into hundreds of thousands.

So the Muslim League got their independent country. Pakistan formally became an Islamic republic in the constitution of 1956, though this was not quite what Jinnah had planned: he kept his palatial 1930s' bungalow on Malabar Hill in Bombay (it is still owned by his family), fondly imagining that he might spend part of his retirement there, which only shows how badly he misread the outcome. Pakistan began as two parts, the eastern one, East Bengal, having nothing in common except religion with the lands to the west that

LEFT

Nehru and Gandhi are blessed by Rama in a painting from the period of the freedom movement. To Nehru's discomfort Gandhi had promised to bring back the 'rule of Rama'.

comprised Baluchis, Punjabis, Pathans and Sindhis. Separated by 2000 miles, East and West Pakistan were never a plausible state, and the East went its own way in the war of 1974, supported by Indira Gandhi's government, becoming Bangladesh, the seventh largest country in the world (Pakistan is the sixth). Meanwhile, a large portion of the Muslim population of British India remained in independent India, though the bitter aftermath of Partition has left many of them an increasingly disadvantaged part of the population. India today is the second largest Muslim country in the world, with around 180 million Muslims. Not surprisingly, many have since wondered what all the suffering was for.

Independent India

Just before midnight on 14 August 1947, Nehru made his long-awaited speech, shot through with pride and regret: 'Long years ago we made a tryst with destiny, and now the time comes when we shall redeem our pledge, not wholly or in full measure, but very substantially. At the stroke of the midnight hour, when the world sleeps, India will awake to life and freedom ...'

Initially, hard times followed Independence. The fiscal balance sheet of the British had seen India, one of the two greatest world economies in the sixteenth century, slump to 3 per cent of world GDP by the early 1900s. The austerities of the early years were exacerbated by the Congress government's self-imposed socialist economic model and Gandhian ethic of self-sufficiency. Famine struck as late as the 1960s. The modernizing of India's 'great tradition' made slow progress until the opening up to foreign investment in the early 1990s. Since then there has been a dramatic rise in India's standard of living and economic power, which is predicted to overtake even the USA by the late 2030s. The twenty-first century, then, will see the old Asian giants returning to their place in history.

An important issue since Independence has been the battle over India's identity. The narrative of Indian history shaped by Congress during the freedom movement was created by Western-educated, English-speaking lawyers and emphasized secularism and Hindu–Muslim unity. Since Independence, and especially in the last two decades, this narrative has been contested, often bitterly. In Nehru's great book *The Discovery of India* (1956) the heroes are enlightened leaders like Akbar, whose idea of India was pluralist and tolerant – hence the importance attached to the Buddhist emperor Ashoka (rediscovered only after 1919), whose lion capital became the emblem of India, and whose wheel of dharma replaced Gandhi's spinning wheel (to the mahatma's displeasure) on the national flag.

But, as always, there are other histories. The majority of India's people are Hindu, and already in the nineteenth century a nascent Hindu nationalist movement saw the British occupation as the catalyst for the end of Muslim power in India and the coming of Hindu rule once the British had gone. The partial failure of the secular ideal in Partition was now to problematize Islam within India for the first time. For if Partition had been on religious grounds, and if Pakistan was an Islamic state, then was India, as Congress asserted, a secular state, or was it really a Hindu country? For Hindu nationalists the answer was obvious. These questions were already insistent at the moment of freedom. Gandhi, who (to Nehru's disquiet) had promised to restore the Ramraj, the golden age of Rama, was assassinated by a Hindu for pandering to Muslims. And this sectarian divide has continued to influence Indian politics

ABOVE

In the shadow of the mahatma: Indira Gandhi and her son Rajiv. Nehru's daughter, Mrs Gandhi suspended democracy in the emergency of 1974, but in a signal display of its resilience Indian democracy was strong enough to throw her out.

over the last twenty years, during which even the terms of India's secular constitution have been called into question.

The main opponent of Congress became a Hindu nationalist party, the BJP, which was founded in 1980 but grew out of earlier 'Hindutva' parties, such as the Hindu Mahasabha (which began in 1915 as a response to the Muslim League), and more hardline organizations, such as the militant RSS (founded 1925) and the VHP (1966). The BJP's rapid rise in the late 1980s was predicated on historical arguments about Hindu–Muslim history (supported and contested by opposing groups of professional historians and archaeologists). They mobilized support around the issue of the destruction of Hindu temples by Muslim rulers in the Middle Ages, focusing in particular on a mosque in Ayodhia alleged to have been built on top of a demolished Hindu temple by Babur, the founder of the Mughal dynasty. Dangerously tapping into communal tensions, the leader of the BJP rode a Toyota truck converted into Rama's chariot on a rabble-rousing pilgrimage across northern India to 'liberate' the birthplace of Ram at Ayodhia. This issue, which, as it turned out, was based on a fantasy of the past, was to threaten the very fabric of the body politic, as Nehru himself had accurately foreseen in 1950. The destruction of the mosque by a mob in 1992 generated an atmosphere of fear and violence that intermittently spilt over into horrific killings, as in Gujarat in 2002. When they became the leaders of the government in the late 1990s the BJP sponsored an archaeological dig on the site of the destroyed mosque to prove the truth of the myth, but, ironically, the dig proved that there had been no significant structure on the site before the Middle Ages: it had not been an early location of the Rama cult. A salutary lesson for those who mix myth and politics.

India Inc.

Unexpectedly, given the increasingly favourable economic climate, the BJP Hindu nationalists were defeated in the 2004 national elections, and the old Congress consensus returned to office to preside over India's economic 'miracle'. These dramatic economic changes had begun in the same year as the Ayodhia disaster, but their long-term effects will reshape our world. To avoid national bankruptcy the then prime minister, Narasimha Rao, dropped Nehru's socialist protectionist economics and opened India up to foreign investment, reformed its capital markets, and deregulated domestic business. Soon Pepsi and Coke could be found on stalls even in India's remotest villages. The final rejection of Gandhi's self-sufficiency ideas has caused some introspection; the biggest Bollywood hit of 2006 even brought the mahatma back to offer guidance

to India's new 'It' generation! Tremendous problems no doubt remain, especially in caste inequalities, rural poverty, environmental degradation and overpopulation. But the world's largest democracy is now firmly set on the path of growth and change, and will go about it in the way that Indian people have always done – adopting what is useful from the outside and holding on tenaciously to the old goals of life inherited from their past.

Unity and diversity

'You have to remember that "India" is your name for us,' says my journalist friend Ravi, expansive and jovial in an extravagantly patterned weekend *kurta*. We are sitting on the steps below the Great Mosque in Delhi: good-natured

ABOVE

Eternal India and its modern incarnation. With population boom and environmental problems, the country's exraordinary growth is not without its dangers, but India has always had an uncanny ability to let the old coexist with the new.

crowds are pouring out after Friday prayers; shoppers are milling around the clothes stalls and *dharbas* (roadside restaurants); boys are selling cheap watches and laminated posters of the Kaaba, the Taj and London's Big Ben. Around us are smoky fires heaped with sizzling kebabs.

Our name for us is Bharat, which has a very different meaning from India. In India time is linear. In Bharat it is circular, mythic. They stand for two different mindsets; and Indian people, even the lowliest, move comfortably between the two. Multiple identities have been part of our history for thousands of years. And these identities are perfectly comfortable with both the ancient and the modern. There is no stigma for a nuclear scientist to worship Ganesh, the elephant-headed god – in fact, we all love him. India has gone through many ups and downs. We have known terrible poverty, but we have great riches from our past. We are comfortable with our culture.

Ravi gestures to the crowds around him:

India is a modern construct – a creation of the British that was made political reality by the freedom movement. Essentially, India was a fantastic, supremely aesthetic and ethical idea dreamt up by a handful of outstanding nationalists, chief among them Nehru, a child of modernism and rationality. He saw the future of India as a grand fusion of West and East. He wanted to cut across ancient allegiances, those encoded memories built up over thousands of years. That past to him was a bar to progress: the iniquities of ignorance, superstition, the caste system and untouchability were all gross inequalities. Democracy and secularism, he thought, would free people from the weight of the past. And despite Partition and secession wars, they did it: they created an allegiance. And about religion surely Nehru was right. In a land of so many religions and 33 million gods, secularism is the only protection for human rights. In any case, is religion the way we should be defined? You know, in the 1991 census, for the first time, they asked a series of questions about religious belief. The interesting thing was, whether Hindus Muslims, Christians, Jains or Parsees, people agreed on most things. In fact, more than 90 per cent of people agreed on what they did and what they believed. Whatever you believe, if your allegiance is to India then you are Indian.

'But there have been scary moments,' I reply. 'The emergency of Indira Gandhi, the Sikh rebellion, Ayodhia. Look at Gujarat in 2002.'

But still it worked. Democracy has taken real root. And perhaps India's economic isolation till the 1990s – Nehru's socialist experiment – played its part. It may have held back the material and social advancement of the Indian people, but it preserved the older ways longer than otherwise could have taken place had there been a headlong rush to modernity and consumerism. When India joined the global market in the 1990s they didn't throw the baby out with the bath water.

14

Further Reading

There's a last ritual at the end of a long filming project – emptying the rucksack for that very last time when you get back home. Spread over the floor is all the traveller's clutter: the mosquito net, the old copies of *India Today*, pilgrim guidebooks, framed pictures and postcards of Hindu gods, chewed-up maps, and cheap dhotis. But with me the biggest pile is always books: all those irresistible purchases from Wheelers of Allahabad, Motilal Banarsidas in the Chowk in Varanasi, or the unmissable bookshops in Delhi's Khan Market. These books (for research but most of all for pleasure), lying on the floor amid the train tickets and cheap posters, and the brown paper packet of cloth from the Madurai tailors' bazaar, draw the eye like familiar friends and recall the delight with which one turned to them on distant shores or mountain tops, in crowded pilgrims lodges, or on late night station platforms. Reflecting on that, it seems to me that not only is there no need in a book of this kind to provide an academic bibliography, it is even undesirable. It is perhaps more helpful to list some books that gave me pleasure and insight, books that I carried with me in my rucksack, and which the reader might wish to carry in his or her own.

First, for a read on the road: *The Picador Book of Modern Indian literature* (ed Amit Chaudhuri, 2002). This is a brilliant idea brilliantly executed, an indispensable introduction to modern Indian literature – and more. It includes a selection of translations from modern vernacular Indian literature, about which most of us, I daresay, are shamefully ignorant.

Other sets of essays: Salman Rushdie and Elizabeth West, *The Vintage Book of Indian Writing 1947–1997* (1997), *India in Mind* (ed Pankaj Mishra, 2005) and that

author's *Temptations of the West* (2006). Amartya Sen's *The Argumentative Indian* (2005) and his *Identity and Violence* (2006) are challenging and humane overviews of India's Great Tradition and its modern dilemmas. Another great pleasure on these travels has been traditional poetry: pride of place goes to the late A.K. Ramanujan's path-breaking translations of early Tamil poetry: *The Interior Landscape* (1967) and *Poems of Love and War* (1985). *The Purananuru*, a wonderful collection of ancient Tamil poems is now out in Penguin (ed G. Hart and H. Heifetz, 2002). The two most famous ancient Tamil epics are also available in Penguin: *Manimekhalai* (tr Alain Danielous, 1996) and *The Cilappatikaram the Tale of an Anklet* (tr R. Parthasarathy 1993). *The Civakacintamani* is untranslated: I used the edition of Book One by James Burgess (1865).

Of the later Tamil devotional poetry (still alive in Tamil Nadu) an old favourite is *Hymns of the Tamil Saivite Saints*, by F. Kingsbury and G. Phillips (1921); see too *Poems to Shiva* by Indira Peterson (1991) and *Songs of the Harsh Devotee* by David Shulman (1990), a guru to all who discover Tamil through translation.

A great Telugu collection of the 16th-century poet Dhurjati is *For the Lord of Animals* (ed H. Heifetz and V. Rao, 1987); wonderful Telugu courtesan songs are in *When God is a Custom* (tr A.K. Ramanujan, V. Rao and D. Shulman, 1994). A Kannada anthology *Speaking of Siva* by A.K. Ramanujan (1973) and his *Songs for the Drowning* (1993) is a great selection of the ninth-century hymns to Vishnu by Nammalvar. These devotional poems are still a living tradition all over India: the works of Kabir, Dadu, Mirabai, Guru Nanak and many others are easily available. In Bengal, Jayadeva's *Gitagovinda* is memorably translated by B. Miller, *Love Song of the Dark Lord* (1977).

On the southern oral tradition try *A Poem at the Right Moment* by V. Rao and D. Shulman (1997), and on oral folktales, *Folktales of India* by A.K. Ramanujan (Penguin, 1994). Many of the great texts of Indian history are easily available in translation: the *Rig Veda* for example by Wendy Doniger (Penguin, 1981), the *Ramayana* in *Rama the Steadfast* by J. and M. Brockington (Penguin, 2006). A fascinating series of essays on the diversity of the tradition is P. Richmann's *Many Ramayanas* (1991).

Modern retellings of the old stories are legion, but *Gods Demons and Others* by the novelist R.K. Narayan (1965 and later eds) is a good railway journey read, along with his longer retellings of the *Ramayana* and *Mahabharata*. The *Kamasutra* is published in Oxford World's Classics by Wendy Doniger and Sudhir Kakar (2002). Babur's Autobiography is published by Penguin (ed Dilip Hero, 2007). Among recent reflections on Indian history is Pankaj Mishra's brilliant *An End to Suffering* (2004) about the Buddha, and the rediscovery, Charles Allen's engaging *The Buddha and the Sahibs* (2002).

General questions of the psychology of Indian culture are treated in many works of Sudhir Kakar, on healing traditions, political and religious violence, and sexuality. His most recent came to my hands too late to use: S. Kakar *The Indians* (2006). The British story too is too vast to go into here: for a judicious recent overview, Lawrence James *The Rise and Fall of the British Empire* (1997), and for the British in the wider context, John Keay *A History of India* (2000). On the Freedom Struggle and Partition there is a vast literature, but a good start is Stanley Wolpert's biographies of Jinnah (1984), Nehru (1996) and Gandhi (2001) and his recent book on Partition *Shameful Flight* (2006), as well as H. Seervai's *Partition of India* (1994). See too Shashi Tharoor's *Nehru*, (2003)

For a broad sweep view of post Independence India, R. Guha's *India After Gandhi* (2007), and for the idea itself, Sunil Khilnani, *The Idea of India* (2003), and Irfan Habib *India – Studies in the History of an Idea* (2004).

Lastly, a few guidebooks and travellers' tales. My old copy of Diana Eck's *Benaras: City of Light* (1983) is falling apart after a dozen visits to that great city and still its pleasures are nowhere near exhausted. *The Last Bungalow* by A.K. Mehrotra (Penguin 2007) is a new anthology on Allahabad's rich modern and mythic history. There are many books on the seven cities of Delhi; Wiliam Dalrymple's *City of Djinns* follows wittily and effortlessly in that great tradition. On Agra and the Taj, Ebba Koch's *The Complete Taj Mahal* (2006) is indispensable and authoritative along with her *Mughal Architecture* (2002). On Mumbai: *Maximum City* by

Suketu Mehta (2004). On Lucknow, among many books by Rosie Llewellyn-Jones are *Lucknow Then and Now* (2003) and *A Fatal Friendship: The Nawabs, The British, and the City of Lucknow* (1985), to be found with other works in her *Lucknow Omnibus* (2001). There is a growing interest in the South now: for example, see *Temple Towns of Tamil Nadu* (ed George Michell, Marg, 1993). I have contributed to a recent study of one great southern religious centre: *Chidambaram* (ed V. Nanda, Marg, 2004) and my *Smile of Murugan* is reissued as *South Indian Journey* (Penguin, 2007). Lastly, Mark Tully *No Full Stops in India* (1994) is the view of a supremely knowledgable outsider and William Dalrymple's *Age of Kali* is an engaging read by the doyen of modern British writers on India.

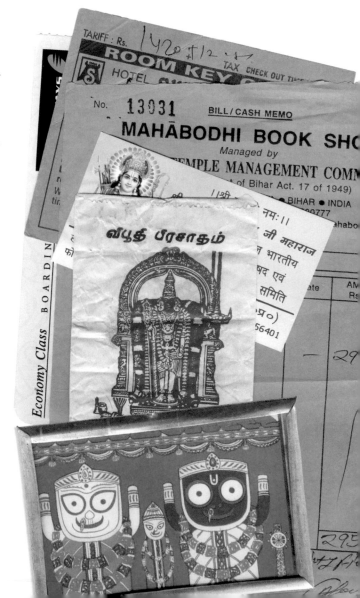

Index

This book is published to accompany the television series entitled *The Story of India*, first broadcast on BBC2 in 2007.

10 9 8 7 6 5 4 3 2

Published in 2007 by BBC Books, an imprint of Ebury Publishing. A Random House Group Company
Copyright © Michael Wood 2007

Commissioning editor: Martin Redfern Project editor: Eleanor Maxfield Copy editor: Patricia Burgess
Designer: Linda Blakemore Picture researcher: Lynda Marshall Production controller: David Brimble

Colour origination, printing and binding by Butler and Tanner, Frome, England